A WORLD OF THINGS TO DO

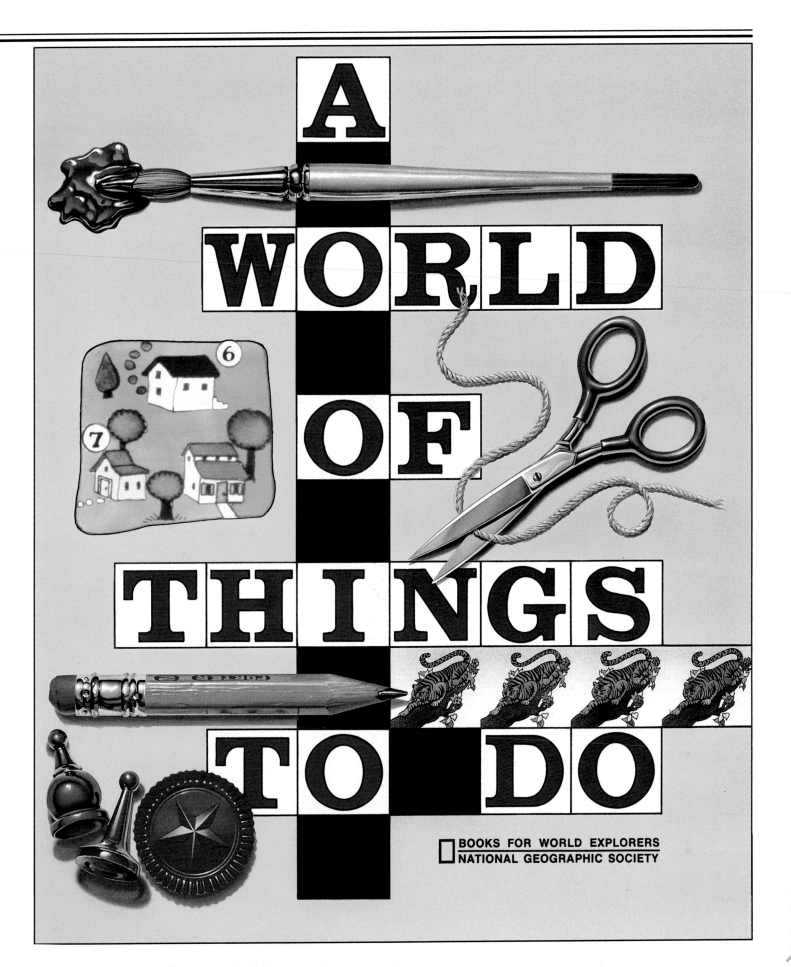

BOOKS FOR WORLD EXPLORERS
NATIONAL GEOGRAPHIC SOCIETY

About this book

Can't think of anything to do today? There's a world of things to do! In these pages you'll find something for just about any occasion.

You'll read about crafts and other activities to enjoy indoors and out, alone and with others. You'll find games both old and new—several played centuries ago in foreign lands...a few favorites of the readers of National Geographic WORLD magazine...and many new ones you can play.

To get the most from *A World of Things To Do*, don't write directly on the pages. Use a pencil and paper, or place a piece of tracing paper over the pages. You also can copy pages on a duplicating machine. That way, you can save your book to enjoy again later or to share.

If any of the puzzles or brainteasers stump you, look on pages 101-103 for the answers.

Contents

Mix and Match

Indoor Fun

Special Days

Brainteasers

COVER: *Shimmering bubbles within a bubble fascinate 11-year-old Joshua McManus, of Santa Cruz, California.*

Outdoor Fun

Games to Go

Give It a Go

Puzzlers

Yummy Treats

Answers   *101 - 103*

Library of Congress CIP data   *104*

Bubble Basics

What better way to spend a rainy, sunny, or any other kind of day than by blowing big, bright, beautiful soap bubbles? You can blow single bubbles or bubble chains or bubbles within bubbles — all with materials you have around the house. Below, 11-year-old Joshua McManus and bubble expert Tom Noddy, both of Santa Cruz, California, create a storm of multicolored bubbles.

If at first you can't create the complex bubbles shown here, don't give up. Bubble-blowing, like any other skill, takes practice and — even more important — patience.

BUBBLE RECIPE
1/3 cup of liquid dishwashing detergent (Some kinds work better than others, so experiment.)
2 quarts of water (at room temperature)

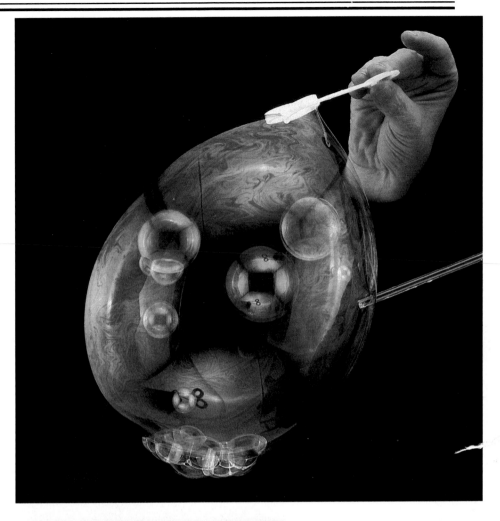

Inexpensive bubble solution you can buy at a grocery or a drugstore makes good bubbles. You can also make your own solution by following the recipe in the bubble at left. Mix the solution in a plastic dishpan, a shallow baking pan, or a large bowl. The recipe makes enough bubbles for a crowd to enjoy. You may want to store some solution in a clean bucket to use later.

Now you'll need some bubble-blowing dippers to use with the solution. You can use regular bubble wands, or you can make wands of your own. Here are some ideas to try.

Almost any empty can makes a good bubble dipper. Make sure it is clean, and has both ends removed. Smooth off any sharp edges. When you dip one end into the bubble solution, a soapy film should form over the opening. If you blow through the other end of the can, a big, beautiful bubble may expand before your eyes.

Add a 2-liter plastic soft-drink bottle to your dipper collection. Soak the bottle in hot water. Then pull away the stiff plastic base. Ask an adult to cut off the end of the bottle with a sharp knife. Dip the now-open end of the bottle into the solution. As you blow through the neck of the bottle, a string of bubbles will poof out the other end.

You can also put some pipe cleaners into bubble-making action. Twist one pipe cleaner into the shape of a figure-8. Wrap one end of another pipe cleaner around the middle of the 8 to form a handle. Make sure there are no sharp ends sticking out. The figure-8 can support larger bubbles than a single circle can.

For bubbles within a bubble (above), blow a large bubble. Dip a straw into the solution and slowly push the straw into the large bubble. Make the smaller bubbles by gently blowing a steady stream of air through the straw.

If you have steady hands and plenty of patience, try making a bubble chain the way Noddy does (left). He holds up the bubble chain with the wand in his left hand and adds new bubbles with the wand in his right hand. Here's an easier way: Catch a bubble on the wand. Then, with the solution-dampened straw, blow another bubble at the base of the first. The bubbles should stick together. Then add another and another and another.

Code-imals

Are you an 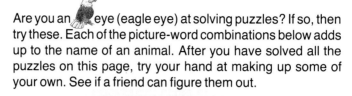eye (eagle eye) at solving puzzles? If so, then try these. Each of the picture-word combinations below adds up to the name of an animal. After you have solved all the puzzles on this page, try your hand at making up some of your own. See if a friend can figure them out.

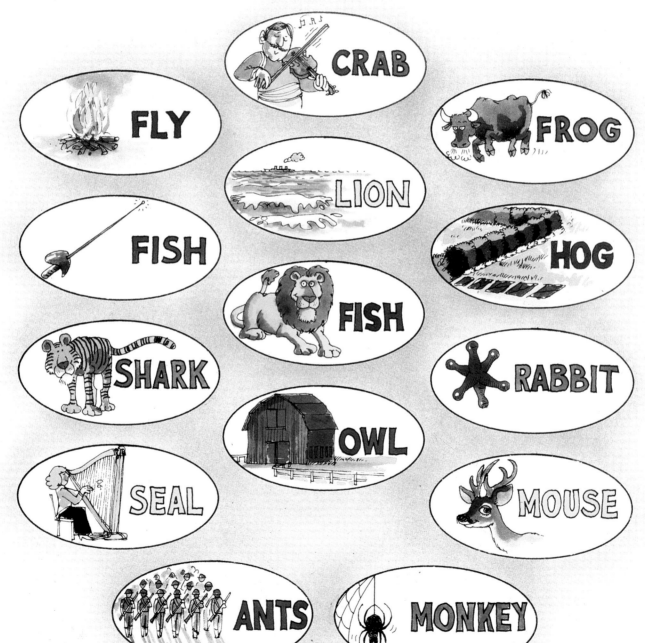

CRAB

FLY

FROG

LION

FISH

HOG

FISH

SHARK

RABBIT

OWL

SEAL

MOUSE

ANTS

MONKEY

Valentine Fun

Here's a way to increase your heartbeat. Look at the word HEART below. How many other words can you think of that contain the letters EA in the same order?

On Valentine Day, invite your friends to play a game everyone will love! For this game, called Hearts Dice, collect six dice. Cover each face of each die with a small square cut from a self-stick mailing label. Print one letter from the word H-E-A-R-T-S on each side of the cube. Prepare the other five dice in the same way. You should have a set of dice like the one above.

Now, you're ready to roll. Decide who goes first. That player rolls all the dice and wins points in this way: H= 5 points; H-E= 10 points; H-E-A = 15 points; H-E-A-R = 20 points; H-E-A-R-T= 25 points; H-E-A-R-T-S = 35 points.

If someone throws double letters (H-H), only one of the letters counts. If someone throws triple letters (E-E-E, for example), only one of the letters counts — unless the letters are H's. If H-H-H is thrown, that player's score goes back to zero.

The player then passes the dice to the player to the left. After ten turns, the player with the highest score wins.

Every February 14, Americans exchange more than 8 million valentines. A small number of these valentines move between friends whose names are anagrams. That means their names have the same letters, but in a different order. Look at the anagrams above, then think of five new ones.

RIDDLE
Question: Why is February 14 the favorite day of the letter V?

RIDDLE
Question: Where does Valentine Day come after the Fourth of July?

Checkers, Anyone?

Feeling . . . challenging? Then challenge a friend to a game of checkers. You don't have to play at home. You can play anywhere. Eleven-year-old Stephanie Dees, of St. Mary's, Georgia, and Chad Carswell, 13, of Ponte Vedra Beach, Florida, (below) are enjoying a game in a park. They're playing on a bandanna checkerboard they made themselves. You can make one, too, by following the directions on page 9.

If you don't want to carry checkers with you, look around for substitutes. You could use pebbles and twigs, bits of colored paper, or coins (with one player using heads and the other player using tails).

To add variety to your playing fun, try some of the other checker games listed on page 10. There are two to play with a friend, and one you can play by yourself.

Here's a classy checkerboard that you can take almost anywhere. To make it, you need a bandanna, a ruler, and a felt-tip marker with permanent black ink.

BANDANNA BOARD
Follow these steps:

1 First, find the center of the bandanna by folding it in half twice, so it's 1/4 of its original size. Crease the center, or faintly mark it with a marker. Be careful not to get ink on anything valuable.

2 Open the bandanna and tape the edges onto a flat surface, such as thick newspaper or a piece of cardboard.

3 Lay the ruler across the bandanna with the ruler's 4-inch (5-inch)* mark on the bandanna's center mark. Make sure the ruler is parallel to the top and bottom edges of the bandanna.

4 Using a felt-tip marker, draw a line 8 (10) inches long, from the end of the ruler through the mark and ending at the 8-inch (10-inch) mark. Then add a dot at each inch ($1\frac{1}{4}$ inch) mark. Draw quickly, so the ink doesn't spread.

5 Lay the ruler up and down so it crosses the line you just drew. Put the ruler's 4-inch (5-inch) mark at the center of the bandanna. Make sure the ruler is parallel to the bandanna's sides.

6 Draw a line 8 (10) inches long and put a dot on the line at each inch ($1\frac{1}{4}$ inch) mark.

7 Draw vertical lines through each dot on the horizontal line. Make each line the same length as the center vertical line and parallel to it.

8 Then, in just the same way, draw horizontal lines through each dot on the vertical line.

9 Where the lines end, draw a line across each side to box in the lines.

10 To complete your board, blacken in every other square.

*To make a larger board, substitute the measurements in parentheses.

FIVE-IN-A-ROW (left)

For this game of strategy for two players, you'll need two different colored sets of 12 checkers. The object of the game is to capture all of your opponent's checkers before your opponent can capture yours. Here are the rules:

1) Choose who goes first. Then take turns placing your checkers, one at a time, on any empty square on the board.

2) When the last checker is in place, take turns moving the checkers around. For one turn, move a checker one square in any direction.

3) To capture your opponent's checker, you must place five of your checkers in a row (in any direction), as the red player has done at left. Whenever you have five in a row, remove from the board — and keep — any one of your opponent's checkers.

4) A player with only four checkers left loses.

5) No jumping is allowed.

CHECKER SOLITAIRE (right)

You can play this game alone. The object is to place eight checkers or other playing pieces on eight squares so that no two pieces are in the same row, column, or diagonal. At right, you can see one way to win, but there are a few more.

CHECKERS FOX AND GEESE (left)

Here's another game for two players. One player uses 12 light-colored checkers called geese. Place these checkers in the same position as in a regular checker game. The other player uses a single dark checker called the fox. Place the fox in the opposite corner, as shown at left. For the fox, the object of the game is to reach the last row on the other side of the board without being captured by the geese. For the geese, the object is to surround the fox so it can't move to that row. Follow these rules:

1) The fox goes first. After that, both players take turns.

2) Players may move only on the dark squares, and only one square at a time.

3) Only the fox may jump, and multiple jumps are permitted.

4) The jumped geese are taken from the board.

April Fool!

If you received a magazine with this scene on the cover, would you be surprised? Readers of *The Saturday Evening Post* probably were—until they noticed it was an April issue. An artist named Norman Rockwell painted this picture as an April Fool joke. He included many strange things—and even signed his name backward. How many odd touches can you spot?

THINK IT OVER

The odds are good that you can figure out these logic games on your own. After you have, think up some new ones — and try them out on an unsuspecting friend.

STARLINE

Study the six-pointed star above. Now, on a piece of scratch paper, try to draw a copy of the star with one continuous line *without lifting your pencil from the paper*. You may cross the same point on a line more than once, but you may not retrace a line.

COIN STACK

Stack a penny, a nickel, a dime, and a quarter on circle A in the same order as in the drawing below. Now, in exactly 15 moves, restack the coins in the same order on spot B, using spot C to help. There are two catches: You can't put a larger size coin on a smaller one, and you can't move more than one coin at a time.

Here are three moves to get you started. You must figure out the other 12 moves.

1) *Move the dime to spot C.*
2) *Put the penny on spot B.*
3) *Put the dime on the penny.*

DIME
PENNY
NICKEL
QUARTER

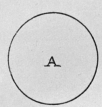
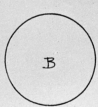
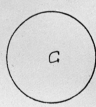

A   B   C

ODD OR EVEN?

A. Pick any two odd numbers. Add them. The answer *always* will be even. True or False?

B. Multiply any number that ends in 5 by any other number ending in 5. The answer also will end in 5. True or False?

C. Subtract any odd number from any other odd number. The answer will be an odd number. True or False?

D. Multiply any odd number by any other odd number. The answer will be an odd number. True or False?

WILL THE BEEST MAKE IT?

Every dry season, antelopes called wildebeests leave the African plain and wander in search of food and water. Some make it. Some don't, because they fall prey to enemies along the way. In this game for two players, each playing piece represents a wildebeest that is struggling to survive.

THE OBJECT OF THE GAME: to capture all of your opponent's wildebeests and remove them from the plain.

HOW TO PLAY: Each player uses 11 playing pieces (or coins, with one player using heads and the other player using tails).

PART 1: Flip a coin to decide who goes first. Then take turns putting the wildebeests on the plain (the grid below). You may not put two of your own wildebeests on adjoining squares.

PART 2: After all the playing pieces are on the board, take turns. On each turn, move one wildebeest one square. You may move it up, down, left, or right, but never diagonally. You may not jump.

HOW TO CAPTURE A WILDEBEEST: Form a wildebeest "herd" by moving three of your pieces into a row. The row may run up, down, or across, but not diagonally. As soon as you have a herd, you may remove one of your opponent's wildebeests from the plain. You may move each one of your playing pieces away from the herd, then move it back—but only once. After that, you must move all three wildebeests away from those three squares before the herd can regroup and capture another wildebeest.

Stamp Stumper

Here's a puzzle to challenge your powers of observation. Grab your pencil and paper and make a list from 1 to 10. Now study the numbered pairs of stamps on these pages. Each pair has something in common. That common element may be found in the words, in the pictures, or in a combination of the two. But it is not the US, the USA, or the value of the stamp.

After you have spotted the common element, look at the stamps in the box at the bottom of these pages. Each one belongs with one of the pairs—but which pair? When you think you have it figured out, write the letter next to a number on your list.

Hint: The answer to number one is A, and the common element is books. Now see if you can match up the rest.

Carter G. Woodson — Black Heritage USA 20c

A Nation of Readers USA 20c

1

STAMP COLLECTING USA 22

Letters Lift Spirits USA 15c

2

Hawaii Statehood 1959-1984 USA 20c

COLORADO 13c usa THE CENTENNIAL STATE

3

Wild pink *Arethusa bulbosa* USA 20c

BLUE JAY USA 20c

4

America's A B C Libraries X Y Z USA 20c Legacies To Mankind
A

Christmas 13c usa
B

FIRST KENTUCKY SETTLEMENT FORT HARROD 1774 1974 us 10c
C

Volunteer lend a hand USA 20c
D

Probing the Planets USA 18c
E

BANKING
US 10c
1875

CREDIT UNION ACT OF 1934
E PLURIBUS UNUM
USA 20c

5

USA 15c
Seeing For Me

USA 22
Frilled Dogwinkle

6

26c AIRMAIL
Shrine of Democracy
USA

George Washington
1732-1982
USA 20c

7

Viking missions to Mars
Expanding human knowledge USA 15c

PIONEER ★ JUPITER
US 10c

8

Grandma Moses
6c U.S. Postage

22
Big Brothers / Big Sisters USA

9

Handcar 1880s
USA 3c

CARE
1946-1971
U.S. 8c

10

P.T.A.
1897
1972
8¢
Parent Teacher Association U.S.

F

NATIONAL ARCHIVES ★ 1934-1984
WHAT IS PAST IS PROLOGUE
USA 20c

G

TAKE A BITE OUT OF CRIME
McGruff The Crime Dog
USA 20¢

H

WHITE OAK
Quercus alba
USA 15c

I

SAVINGS AND LOANS
SAVE
USA 18¢

J

START A COLLECTION

The last time you cleaned out your closet, did you come across those old baseball cards you gathered last year . . . or the handful of seashells you picked up on the beach . . . or maybe the car models that were in your Christmas stocking? If so, you may already have a base for building a collection.

Collecting doesn't have to cost much money, and it may launch you into a hobby you can enjoy for the rest of your life.

Getting started

First, decide what you want—and can afford—to collect. You don't need much money to start a penny collection, but you'll need some income to collect model airplanes. There are a lot of other ideas on these pages.

Once you decide what interests you, read all you can about it. Your public library has books and magazines not only on your specific interest, but also on collecting in general.

Building blocks

Objects to start—or add to—your collection may be hiding anywhere. If you're collecting such things as model cars or tin soldiers, visit your local dime store, hobby shop, or toy store. Watch for flea markets, garage sales, and estate sales. You may find that, somewhere near you, people regularly gather at fairs or meets to swap, buy, and sell what you're collecting. Fairs also are good places to trade information with experts.

Keeping Track

Organize your collection so you know what you have and what you're missing. Then make an up-to-date card file. Before you visit a show or a flea market, have a list handy of what you're missing.

Are you serious?

If you want to build a collection that may grow more valuable with time, collect only items in tiptop condition—and keep them that way.

HOW BIG IS A MILLION?

A computer can tell you. Computers can count to any number — if you have the time to wait.

You can tell most personal computers to count to a million by typing in the following BASIC program. After you "save" the program, type the word "run." The computer will flash the question "TO WHAT NUMBER WOULD YOU LIKE ME TO COUNT?" Type in 1000000 . . . and then wait. It will take a long, long time.

```
NEW
10 GOTO 70
20 FOR I = 1 TO A
30 PRINT I
40 NEXT I
50 PRINT "TYPE THE WORD RUN TO
COUNT AGAIN."
60 GOTO 90
70 INPUT "TO WHAT NUMBER WOULD
YOU LIKE ME TO COUNT?";A
80 GOTO 20
90 END
SAVE MILLION
```

NIM

People have been playing the game of NIM for centuries. In fact, experts believe that NIM originated in ancient China, and is one of the oldest two-player games in the world. It's just as challenging today. Here's how to play: Set up four rows of objects. Pebbles work well. Put a different number of pebbles in each row. For example, put seven pebbles in row one, five in row two, three in row three, and one in row four. Now, take turns removing pebbles until you have removed them all. The player who takes the last pebble wins.

NIM has only two rules:
1) A player may remove any number of pebbles during a turn, but from only one row.
2) A player may not skip a move or remove zero pebbles during a turn.

You can also play NIM using a computer as the other player. First type in the program below. After you "save" it, type the word "run." The computer will tell you how to play.

```
NEW
100 FOR A = 1 TO 25: PRINT : NEXT A :
PRINT TAB(20);"NIM" : FOR A = 1 TO 5 :
PRINT : NEXT A
110 DIM A(100),B(100,10),D(2)
120 PRINT "THIS IS THE GAME OF NIM."
130 PRINT "DO YOU WANT TO READ
SOME INSTRUCTIONS?";
140 INPUT " " ; YN$
150 IF YN$ ="NO" THEN 280
160 IF YN$ ="no" THEN 280
170 IF YN$ ="YES" THEN 210
180 IF YN$ ="yes" THEN 210
190 PRINT "PLEASE ANSWER YES OR
NO.": PRINT
200 GOTO 240
210 PRINT : PRINT "THE GAME IS
PLAYED WITH A NUMBER OF":PRINT
"PILES OF OBJECTS."
220 PRINT : PRINT "RULES:"
230 PRINT :"1. A PLAYER MAY REMOVE
ANY NUMBER OF PEBBLES DURING A
TURN, BUT FROM ONLY ONE ROW."
240 PRINT "2. A PLAYER MAY NOT SKIP
A MOVE OR": PRINT "REMOVE ZERO
OBJECTS DURING A TURN."
250 PRINT "ON EACH OF ITS TURNS,
THE MACHINE PLAYS BY THE SAME
RULES."
260 PRINT "THE MACHINE WILL SHOW
ITS MOVE BY LISTING EACH PILE AND
THE NUMBER OF"
270 PRINT "OBJECTS REMAINING IN
THE PILES AFTER": PRINT "EACH OF
ITS MOVES."
280 FOR A=1 TO 6:PRINT:NEXT A
290 PRINT "ENTER THE NUMBER 1 TO
WIN BY TAKING THE LAST" : PRINT
"OBJECT OR THE NUMBER 2
TO WIN BY AVOIDING IT.";
300 INPUT " ";W
310 IF W=1 THEN 330
320 IF W<>2 THEN 290
330 PRINT : PRINT "ENTER THE
NUMBER OF PILES.:";
340 INPUT " ";N
350 IF N>100 THEN 330
360 IF N<1 THEN 330
370 IF N<>INT(N) THEN 330
380 PRINT : PRINT "ENTER THE
NUMBER OF OBJECTS IN EACH:PRINT
"PILE."
390 FOR I=1 TO N
400 PRINT I":";
410 INPUT " " ; A(I)
420 IF A(I)>2000 THEN 400
430 IF A(I)<1 THEN 400
440 IF A(I)<>INT(A(I)) THEN 400
450 NEXT I
460 PRINT "DO YOU WANT TO MOVE
FIRST?";
470 INPUT " ";YN$
480 IF YN$ = "YES" THEN 1290
490 IF YN$ = "yes" THEN 1290
500 IF YN$ = "NO" THEN 540
510 IF YN$ = "no" THEN 540
520 PRINT "PLEASE ANSWER YES OR
NO.": PRINT
530 GOTO 460
540 IF W=1 THEN 780
550 LET C=0
560 FOR I=1 TO N
570 IF A(I)=0 THEN 610
580 LET C=C+1
590 IF C=3 THEN 680
600 LET D(C)=I
610 NEXT I
620 IF C=2 THEN 760
630 IF A(D(1))>1 THEN 660
640 PRINT "THE MACHINE LOSES.":
PRINT
650 GOTO 1480
660 PRINT "THE MACHINE WINS.":
PRINT
670 GOTO 1480
680 LET C=0
690 FOR I=1 TO N
700 IF A(1)>1 THEN 780
710 IF A(1)=0 THEN 730
720 LET C=C+1
730 NEXT I
740 IF C/2<>INT(C/2) THEN 640
750 GOTO 780
760 IF A(D(1))=1 THEN 660
```

```
770 IF A(D(2))=1 THEN 660
780 FOR I=1 TO N
790 LET E=A(I)
800 FOR J=0 TO 10
810 LET F=E/2
820 LET B(I,J)=2*(F-INT(F))
830 LET E=INT(F)
840 NEXT J
850 NEXT I
860 FOR J=10 TO 0 STEP -1
870 LET C=0
880 LET H=0
890 FOR I=1 TO N
900 IF B(I,J)=0 THEN 950
910 LET C=C+1
920 IF A(I)<=H THEN 950
930 LET H=A(I)
940 LET G=I
950 NEXT I
960 IF C/2<>INT(C/2) THEN 1030
970 NEXT J
980 LET E=INT(N*RND(1)+1)
990 IF A(E)=C THEN 980
1000 LET F=INT(A(E)*RND(1)+1)
1010 LET A(E)=A(E)-F
1020 GOTO 1220
1030 LET A(G)=0
1040 FOR J=0 TO 10
1050 LET B(G,J)=0
1060 LET C=0
1070 FOR I=1 TO N
1080 IF B(I,J)=0 THEN 1100
1090 LET C=C+1
1100 NEXT I
1110 LET A(G)=A(G)+2*(C/2-
INT(C/2))*2^J
1120 NEXT J
1130 IF W=1 THEN 1220
1140 LET C=0
1150 FOR I=1 TO N
1160 IF A(I)>1 THEN 1220
1170 IF A(I)=0 THEN 1190
1180 LET C=C+1
1190 NEXT I
1200 IF C/2<>INT(C/2) THEN 1220
1210 LET A(G)=1-A(G)
1220 PRINT : PRINT "PILE SIZE"
1230 FOR I=1 TO N
1240 PRINT I ":";: IF A(I) >=0 THEN FOR
A = 1 TO A(I): PRINT "*";: NEXT A
1250 PRINT:NEXT I
1260 IF W=2 THEN 1290
1270 GOSUB 1410
1280 IF Z=1 THEN 660
1290 PRINT "YOUR MOVE. TYPE THE
PILE, A COMMA,":PRINT "AND THE
NUMBER TO BE REMOVED.";
1300 INPUT " "; X,Y
1310 IF X>N THEN 1290
1320 IF X<1 THEN 1290
1330 IF X<>INT(X) THEN 1290
1340 IF Y>A(X) THEN 1290
1350 IF Y<1 THEN 1290
1360 IF Y<>INT(Y) THEN 1290
1370 LET A(X)=A(X)-Y
1380 GOSUB 1410
1390 IF Z=1 THEN 640
1400 GOTO 540
1410 LET Z=0
1420 FOR I=1 TO N
1430 IF A(I)=0 THEN 1450
1440 RETURN
1450 NEXT I
1460 LET Z=1
1470 RETURN
1480 PRINT "DO YOU WANT TO PLAY
ANOTHER GAME?";
1490 INPUT " ";YN$
1500 IF YN$="YES" THEN 1560
1510 IF YN$="yes" THEN 1560
1520 IF YN$="NO" THEN 1570
1530 IF YN$="no" THEN 1570
1540 PRINT "PLEASE ANSWER YES OR
NO.": PRINT
1550 GOTO 1480
1560 GOTO 280
1570 END
SAVE NIM
```

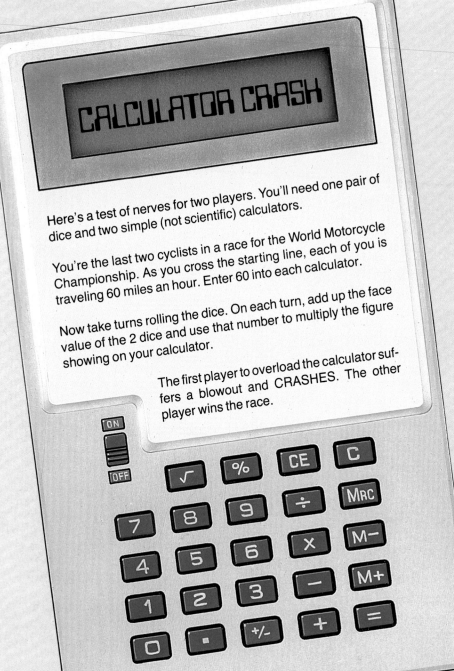

CALCULATOR CRASH

Here's a test of nerves for two players. You'll need one pair of dice and two simple (not scientific) calculators.

You're the last two cyclists in a race for the World Motorcycle Championship. As you cross the starting line, each of you is traveling 60 miles an hour. Enter 60 into each calculator.

Now take turns rolling the dice. On each turn, add up the face value of the 2 dice and use that number to multiply the figure showing on your calculator.

The first player to overload the calculator suffers a blowout and CRASHES. The other player wins the race.

Planning sand pictures, Robert Finnigan and Debbie Frakes study designs. The table holds supplies: sand, spoons, brushes, and clean, dry containers.

Thin layers of sand form the bottom part of Robert's design. He spreads each sand layer evenly around the jar and works carefully, to avoid mixing colors.

Make a picture in a jar with Sand

Robert levels sand with his brush, while Debbie spoons more layers into her jar. They brush away any sand grains that stick to the sides.

To vary his design, Robert presses the end of a paintbrush against the jar and pushes the brush down (left). Sand also moves down, forming a pattern with points.

Finished work brings smiles to the faces of the artists (above). Both hold their jars carefully. The slightest movement could shift the sand and ruin the design.

A sand face peers through the side of a clear plastic planter (below). Once you have learned the basics of sand painting, you can try harder designs — an animal or a scene. Just let your imagination go!

By adding potting soil, Robert turns his sand design into a garden. Plants that grow slowly and need very little water do well in sand gardens. Many people prefer cactus plants. When you water your plant, sprinkle it lightly so you don't spoil the sand design.

Painting with loose sand? It may sound impossible, but it isn't. Simply take a glass jar and add colored sand, plus a little imagination. You can create designs like the ones on these pages. Robert Finnigan, 13, and Debbie Frakes, 13, both of McLean, Virginia, show you how.

Making pictures in sand is an old art. For centuries, Navajo Indians have "painted" scenes by sprinkling crushed stones of different colors onto a background of smooth sand. The Indians thought such designs could drive out evil spirits and heal sick people.

You can make a sand painting in a jar by following the instructions on these pages. Here are some hints to help you get started:

Use only nontoxic, colorfast sand. You can buy it in small packages in hardware and variety stores. Choose clear, sturdy containers that won't break from the weight of the sand. Pickle jars are good. If you plan to top off your design with a plant, select a container with a wide mouth.

TOP SECRET

Want to send a secret message that only your best friend can read? The codes on these pages make sending secrets a snap.

HIDE YOUR MESSAGE BEHIND A MASK

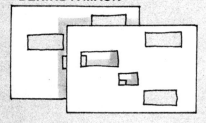

Put two pieces of paper together and cut identical windows in both. Mark "top" on each. Give one to a friend. Put your "mask" over a blank paper and write in the windows. Remove the "mask" and add more words to hide your message. Your friend can read the message using the other mask.

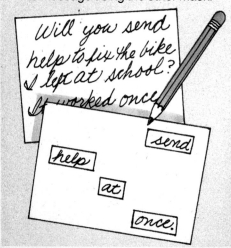

SEMAPHORE

Messages sometimes travel between ships by semaphore — a signaling system using two flags. Held in different positions, the flags stand for letters. You can send these signals on paper — by drawing stick figures with arms set like the hands of a clock.

Here's an easy code that takes only a ruler and a piece of paper. Lay the ruler across the paper. Print your message in capital letters, placing each letter above the inch and the half-inch marks on the ruler. Circle the last letter of your message. Then, to confuse snoopers, fill in other letters between the letters of

your message so that they form other words. The words shouldn't have anything to do with the real message.

To read the message, your friend places a ruler under the line of words, with the circled letter over an inch or a half-inch mark and copies off the letters at each inch and half-inch interval.

SCRAMBLED LETTERS

Cut a paper rectangle and a strip that slides through it (above). Write the alphabet from A to Z on the rectangle and write it twice from Z to A on the strip. Space both alphabets alike. Choose a key letter and position it beneath the A. Write your message, but substitute letters from the strip for the real ones. The key letter for the message at right is M.

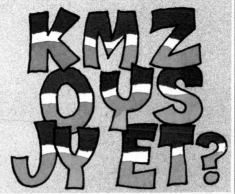

FOLD SOME PAPER

You can hide a message just by folding paper. Try the two ways shown here. Fold the paper in half (above). Then fold the halves back to make panels. Write the message so the words read across the panels. Jumble the message with extra words.

NUMBER SWITCH

To make an easy number code, substitute a number for every letter in the alphabet. Begin with the number one for the letter A, two for B, and so on. Can you decode the message above?

For a different number code, put the alphabet in a box (above). Put either I and J or Y and Z together in one box. Write each letter as a two-digit number: A=11, B=12, C=13, and so on.

You can also fold a piece of paper into quarters (above) and write a vertical message on the creases. Then add a false message around the real one.

BUILD A PIGPEN OR A BOX

 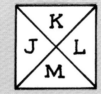

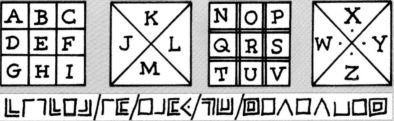

Civil War soldiers used pigpens and boxes to send secret messages. A typical pigpen (above) substitutes a symbol for each letter. Your friend will need a copy of your pigpen design to decipher your message. Can you read the sentence above?

"Route Ciphers" (right) put messages in boxes. To make one, mark your "route" in a blank box. Give a copy of the marked box to your friend. Write your message in the box so it follows the route. For a long message, use two boxes. Then copy the letters from left to right, top row to bottom row. Your friend will copy the letters in the same order, then read the message using your route. Three route ciphers are shown at right. Read the top one from bottom to top in each row.

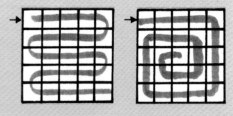

Cook a Foreign Feast

Learning to cook a fancy dinner can be fun! And you don't have to wait until you grow up to start learning how to do it. "Kids can cook just about anything if they are given a chance," says Sandra Bresnick.

Mrs. Bresnick should know. At her Creative Cooking School, in Bethesda, Maryland, she taught cooking to children as well as to adults. She showed the five youngsters on the opposite page how to prepare an international feast. Each dish comes from a different part of the world. On the map, you can see where all the dishes come from.

The meal the group prepared included chicken tandoori (tan-DOOR-ee) from India, broiled tomatoes from Italy, cucumber-and-yogurt salad from Greece, and chocolate mousse (MOOSE) from France. The meal was topped off with a pineapple drink from Puerto Rico.

After the young cooks had spent nearly two hours peeling, chopping, whipping, and mixing, dinner was finally ready. Then came the best part of their cooking class — eating what they had prepared. What did they think of the dishes they had created?

"The food was worth waiting for," said Ricky Sluss, 12, of Centreville, Virginia.

To cook a meal like the one these youngsters prepared, follow the directions on the following pages. The recipe for each dish is given, plus a list of cooking tips.

Measuring bread crumbs, Ricky Sluss, 12, of Centreville, Virginia, helps prepare Italian-style broiled tomatoes (above). Ricky and four other young cooks prepared an international meal as part of a cooking class.

Cooking teacher Sandra Bresnick shows Akiko Herron, 9, of Great Falls, Virginia, the safe way to chop vegetables (right). "Keep the sharp edge of the knife away from your fingers," Mrs. Bresnick warns.

Young cooks display the dishes from around the world that they have prepared. Allison Atlas, 10, of Bethesda, Maryland, holds a flowerpot full of chocolate mousse, bottom left. Akiko shows off a pineapple drink, bottom right. Ricky holds a cucumber-and-yogurt salad, top left. Fred Krumbhaar, 10, of Washington, D. C., displays the main course, chicken tandoori, center. Mike Karlin, 12, of Bethesda, holds a plate of broiled tomatoes, top right. All five cooks helped make each dish.

RECIPES

Safety Tips

1 Always ask for permission to use the kitchen before you start cooking.

2 Ask an adult to help you whenever you must use a sharp knife, a can opener, a blender, or a mixer, or whenever you cook with anything hot, such as the top of the stove, the oven, or the broiler.

3 Turn the handles of all pans on the stove away from the front. That way you won't catch them with your clothes and tip them over. Don't place a handle over a burner that's on.

4 Turn off and unplug the mixer before you put in or take out the beaters.

5 Use thick, dry pot holders to pick up hot dishes so you won't burn your hands.

Cook's Checklist

1 Wash your hands before you start to cook. Put on a clean apron. If your hair is long, tie it back.

2 Read each recipe all the way through. If there's something you don't understand, ask an adult.

3 Get out all the ingredients and utensils listed in the recipe. Wash all the fruits and vegetables. As soon as you finish using a refrigerated product, put it back in the refrigerator so it won't spoil.

4 Make sure all appliances are turned off after you finish cooking. Wash the dishes and clean up the area where you've been working.

Cooking Terms

 Double boiler: two pans that fit together, one on top of the other. The bottom pan holds water. The top pan holds the food. When the water is heated, it cooks the food without burning it.

 Fold: to mix ingredients with a slow and gentle circular motion. Mix from the bottom of the bowl to the top.

 **Grate:** to break a solid food, such as a carrot, into small pieces by rubbing it against the rough surface of a grater.

 Mince: to cut food into tiny pieces.

Stiff peaks: small peaks that stand up on top of whipped mixtures.

Mike samples a fresh pineapple cooler (left).

PINEAPPLE COOLER

PUERTO RICO

Pineapples and coconuts both grow on the sunny island of Puerto Rico. The people of Puerto Rico make a refreshing drink by combining these two fruits. To make pineapple coolers for your friends, you'll need the following ingredients for each serving:

1/2 cup of cream of coconut (You can buy this in most grocery stores.)

1 cup of unsweetened pineapple juice

2 cups of crushed ice (To make crushed ice, empty a tray of ice cubes into a plastic storage bag. Tie the bag shut, and crush the cubes with a hammer. Do this on a cutting board. Then measure out the two cups.)

• Put all of the ingredients into a blender. Blend for about one minute. (If you don't have a blender, put the ingredients in a pitcher and stir briskly for two minutes. You can also pour the mixture into a large jar with a tight-fitting top and shake it vigorously for one minute.)

• Pour the mixture into a drinking glass and decorate with cubes of fruit, such as bananas and cherries. Spear the fruit on a straw or a stirrer.

CHOCOLATE MOUSSE

FRANCE

In French, the word *mousse* means frothy and foamy. Chocolate mousse is a frothy and foamy dessert. Here's what you'll need to make chocolate mousse for six people:

12 ounces of semi-sweet chocolate bits
2 whole eggs
4 egg yolks
4 egg whites
2 teaspoons of vanilla
2 cups of heavy cream
2 teaspoons of powdered sugar
6 strawberries (optional)

• Melt the chocolate bits in a double boiler. Remove the melted chocolate from the heat.
• Separate the whites from the yolks of four eggs. (Ask an adult to show you how to do this, if you've never done it.)
• Crack the two whole eggs and add them to the four yolks. Beat the whole eggs and the yolks together with a fork. Stir them into the melted chocolate. Stir the mixture until all of it becomes the same color.
• Beat the four egg whites with an electric mixer until stiff peaks form.
• Gently fold the egg whites into the chocolate mixture.
• Whip 3/4 cup of heavy cream until it forms stiff peaks. Fold it into the chocolate mixture. Pour the mixture into individual serving bowls and refrigerate for at least two hours.

• When the mousse is firm, whip the rest of the heavy cream until it forms peaks. Stir the vanilla and sugar into the whipped cream.
• Put the whipped cream on top of the mousse. Top each serving with a strawberry, if you wish.

With a circular motion, Mike folds beaten egg whites and whipped cream into a mousse.

CUCUMBER-AND-YOGURT SALAD

GREECE

Here's a salad often eaten in Greece. To make this salad, which serves six people, you'll need:

1 carton of plain yogurt (8 ounces)
2 cucumbers, peeled and sliced
1 small clove of garlic, minced
1 tablespoon of olive oil
2 tablespoons of lemon juice
1/2 cup of grated carrots
1 head of red cabbage

• Lightly salt the cucumbers and set them aside for ten minutes.
• Pour the yogurt into a bowl. Mix in the garlic, olive oil, and lemon juice.
• Rinse the cucumbers and drain them. Add them to the yogurt mixture.
• Serve on red cabbage leaves. Sprinkle grated carrots on top.

BROILED TOMATOES

ITALY

The Italians have created many dishes using tomatoes. To make this Italian dish for six people, you'll need:

6 large ripe tomatoes
3/4 cup of bread crumbs
1/3 stick of melted butter or margarine
12 slices of mozzarella cheese or 12 tablespoons of grated Parmesan cheese
Oregano

- Cut each tomato in half. Place the tomato halves, cut sides up, in an oven-proof pan.

- If you are using mozzarella cheese, put one slice on top of each of the tomato halves.

- Mix together the bread crumbs and melted butter. Add the Parmesan cheese if you are using it. Spread the mixture evenly over the tomato halves.

- Sprinkle the tomatoes with oregano. Put them under the broiler, about 4 to 6 inches away from the heat source. Cook them for 5 to 10 minutes, until the tops are puffy and lightly browned.

CHICKEN TANDOORI

INDIA

In northern India, chicken is often cooked in a *tandoor* — a clay oven that is usually buried in the ground. A charcoal fire in the bottom of the tandoor cooks the chicken and gives it a special flavor. You probably don't have a tandoor to use, but here is a way to get almost the same results. To make chicken tandoori for six people, you will need:

2 packages of cut-up chicken (about 12 pieces)
2 cups of onions, diced — chopped into pieces the size of a pea
1 clove of garlic
2 green peppers, chopped, with the seeds and white pulp removed
2 tomatoes, chopped
2 teaspoons of salt
1 tablespoon each of curry powder, ground dried coriander, and ground cumin
1 teaspoon of tumeric
1/2 teaspoon of cinnamon
1 teaspoon of ground black pepper
1/2 cup of melted butter or margarine
2 chicken-flavored bouillon cubes
1 package of white rice (optional)

Fred and Mike put chicken tandoori into the oven (left).

Akiko enjoys the dinner she and the other cooks have prepared.

- Preheat the oven to 375 degrees.
- Rinse the chicken pieces under cold, running water.
- Put a whole garlic bud, made up of several cloves of garlic, on the table or counter. Hit the garlic bud with the heel of your hand so the cloves break apart. Peel one clove and chop it into very tiny pieces.
- Arrange the chicken pieces, skin side up, in a shallow baking pan. Pour the butter or margarine over them.
- Sprinkle the chicken with the chopped onion, garlic, green peppers, tomatoes, salt, curry powder, coriander, cumin, tumeric, cinnamon, and black pepper.
- Dissolve two chicken-flavored bouillon cubes in two cups of hot water. (You can also use canned chicken broth, chicken stock someone has made, or plain water.)
- Add the liquid to the baking pan and put the pan in the preheated oven. Bake the chicken for 50 minutes. (The chicken may be served on steamed white rice. Prepare the rice according to the directions on the package.)

TUNNEL CRAWL. *Open both ends of a large cardboard box to make a tunnel. Crawl through the box. Charissa Recinto, 10, of Annandale, Virginia, uses her elbows to pull the rest of her body along (left).*

CRAB CRAWL. *Lie on your back. Lift your body on your hands and feet and walk backward 10 paces.*

LIMBO. *Suspend a pole between two lawn chairs. Face the pole and bend backward. Try to walk under the pole without touching it, as Kristin Reich, 9, of Falls Church, Virginia, does here. To make a harder obstacle, lower the pole.*

JUMP ROPE. *Grab a jump rope. Twirl the rope and jump it ten times. Keep both feet together as you jump. Now go back to the crab crawl.*

DRIBBLING. *Set up four field markers in a zigzag course. Then dribble a soccer ball through the course.*

TIRE TREADING. *Set up two lines of tires and quickly step from tire to tire.*

SIDEWALK HOP. *Chalk a figure the size and shape of a baseball home plate. Stand on two corners of the figure. Jump to the next two corners, then hop on one foot to the point, as Stephen Kenney, 10, of Falls Church, does here. Repeat five times.*

BUILD AN OBSTACLE COURSE

Bored with jungle gyms, swings, and slides? Tired of the same old summer games? Why not set up an obstacle course that you and your friends can use? An obstacle course is fun to design and set up. As you master it, you'll develop some useful physical skills.

All you need for your course are a few things to use as obstacles, some space in a yard, a playground, or a vacant lot, and plenty of imagination. First, think of activities that require flexibility, balance, or strength. The pictures here will give you some ideas. Then collect the equipment. If you don't have some of the things shown, substitute other things. Now you're ready to set up your course and give it a try. You and a friend should take turns timing each other. Run the course as quickly as you can. After you can run one set of obstacles easily, try making the course harder.

GEOJUMBLE

Where in the United States can you find the highest point above sea level?

Finding the answer to the question above takes a lot of unscrambling. So grab a pencil and paper and make a list from one to five.

First, you must unscramble each of the words below. Each one describes a familiar physical feature of the earth, such as a body of water.

After you have unscrambled all the words, follow the directions beneath each one. You will have another scrambled word.

When you unscramble that word, you'll have the answer!

1. **K E A L**
(Use the third letter)

2. **C O O N V A L**
(Use the third letter)

3. **S P M A W**
(Use the first and the third letters)

4. **S N I L A D**
(Use the fourth letter)

5. **L L A Y V E**
(Use the second letter)

Know Your Globe

CHECK OUT THESE FANCY CATS!

Can you figure out the names of these cat breeds? Each name takes you somewhere in the world. You'll find the names listed below.

1) This cat comes from an island in the Irish Sea. Though its tail is short or missing, its name is longer — by an X — than the name of its home.

2) This lion-colored cat may have purred for pharoahs, but it's named after another ancient African country.

3) First appearing in New England, this fluffy cat has a tail resembling the one worn by a masked trash-can bandit.

4) If you want to give this steely looking cat a name that fits its original birthplace, call it Boris or Natasha.

5) A lean, talkative climber, this favorite of many people originated in the Asian country now called Thailand.

6) A country by Thailand on the Bay of Bengal may have been the home of this brown cat that shares its name.

7) To figure out this cat, take the shape of #8, give it the coloring of #5, and name it after a tall mountain range.

8) Silky-haired and gentle, this cat came from the Middle East. Its name recalls the land now called Iran.

9) First bred in bagpipe country north of England, this cat has small ears that bend forward at the tip.

10) For this cat's name, think of taffy — or of the star of Thanksgiving dinner. Your fuzzy sweater doesn't contain its fur. That's from sheep or rabbits or goats.

Breeds: Abyssinian, Burmese, Maine coon, Manx, Persian, Siamese, Russian blue, Himalayan, Turkish Angora, Scottish fold

WHERE IN THE U.S.A.?

In the circles at right are sections of actual maps from around the United States. Can you figure out the state or federal district that each map shows?

1

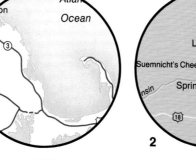

2

3

4

5

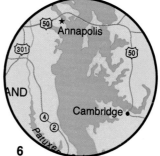

6

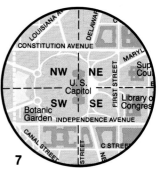

7

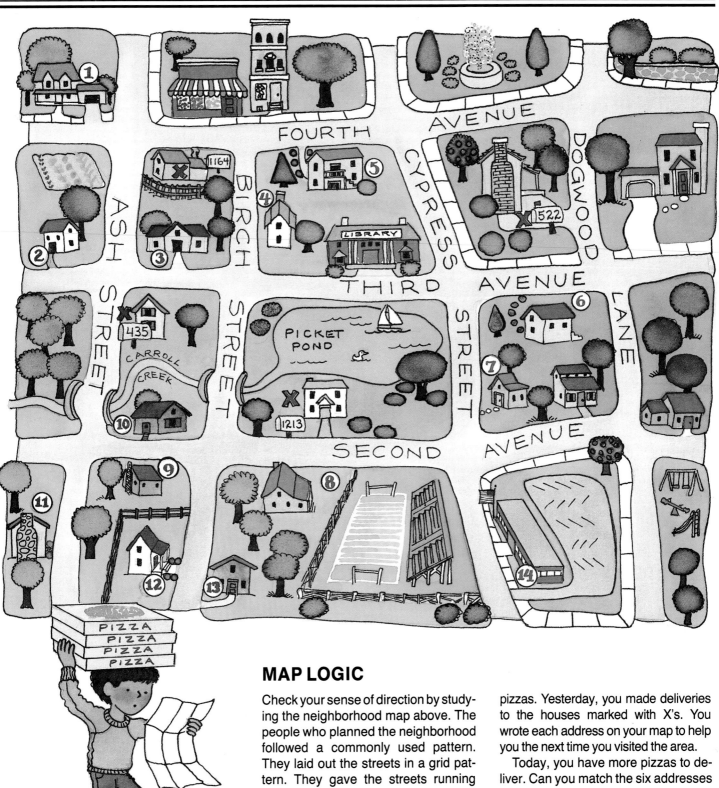

MAP LOGIC

Check your sense of direction by studying the neighborhood map above. The people who planned the neighborhood followed a commonly used pattern. They laid out the streets in a grid pattern. They gave the streets running east and west numbers, and they gave the streets running north and south names. The houses on one side of the street have even numbers, and those on the other side have odd numbers. The numbers generally are the same from street to street.

You work after school delivering pizzas. Yesterday, you made deliveries to the houses marked with X's. You wrote each address on your map to help you the next time you visited the area.

Today, you have more pizzas to deliver. Can you match the six addresses below with some of the red numbers on the map?

423 Cypress Street
1156 Second Avenue
340 Ash Street
1075 Fourth Avenue
527 Birch Street
1117 Third Avenue

MAGIC·TRICKS
to amaze your friends

MIND READING

Tell your friends that you can read minds. Prove it by spreading out nine magazines as shown below. Turn your back. Ask someone to touch one of the magazines and then step away.

Now turn around. Tell everyone to concentrate on the correct magazine, but not to look directly at it.

Your assistant, who also knows how to do the trick, touches a magazine with a measuring stick and asks, "Is it this one?" You answer "No." You answer "Yes" only when the pointer finally touches the right magazine.

The secret is in *where* your assistant touches the *first* magazine. Imagine that the cover is divided into nine sections. The top left corner of the cover means that the correct magazine is the top left one. The middle of the cover means the middle magazine. In the drawing above, the pointer tells the "mind reader" that the correct magazine is at the bottom right.

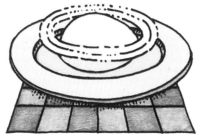

EGGS-CITEMENT

You're such a great magician that you have power to make an egg spin. The secret is that only hard-boiled eggs spin. Before your performance, put a tiny dot on the shell of the only hard-boiled egg in a bowl of eggs. Pick out the marked egg and spin it. Ask a friend to try another egg. Your friend's egg won't spin. It will wobble.

MAGIC TOOTHPICK

Unfold a handkerchief and give it a good shake to show there's nothing hidden inside. Spread the handkerchief across your palm and place a toothpick on it.

Now fold the handkerchief and hold it so you can feel the toothpick through the cloth. Invite someone to break the toothpick. With a dramatic flourish, shake the handkerchief so the toothpick tumbles out — in one piece!

Here's how to do the trick: Before your performance, hide a toothpick inside the hem of the handkerchief. During the trick, hold the handkerchief so the toothpick hidden in the hem is the one that gets broken.

BLACKS AND REDS

It's easy to pick a certain card out of a deck — if you arrange the deck beforehand. Sort the cards so all the black ones are together and all the red ones are together.

Ask someone to pick a card and look at it. Watch which half of the deck the card comes from. Take the card back and slide it into the other half of the deck. To find the card, look for one that doesn't match the color of the cards around it.

STOP THE CLOCK

Ask a friend to choose a number on a clock and *not* to tell what the number is. *You* find the number!

Turn the clock so your friend can't see it. Then explain that while you tap the clock face with your pencil, your friend should count each tap silently, starting with the number after the chosen one. If the number is 9, for example, your friend should start counting with 10. Instead of the count of 20, your friend should say "Stop!"

To make the trick work, you must count silently, too. Tap any numbers you like for the first *seven* taps. On the eighth tap, touch 12. After that, tap backward (11, 10, 9, and so on) until your friend says "Stop." Your pencil will be on the correct number.

PICK A CARD

Here's another way to pick a card out of a deck.

You must remember the card on the bottom of the deck. Fan out the deck.

Ask a friend to pick a card and to look at it carefully. Take the top half of the deck in your left hand and the bottom half in your right hand. Hold out the left-hand pile and tell your friend to put the card on top of it. Then put the cards in your right hand on the others.

Spread the cards again. Your friend's card will be the one under the card that was on the bottom when you began the trick.

FOUR-SIDED CARD

Here's an easy card trick. Hold up a card. With practice, you can make one card appear to have four sides!

Cut out a piece of cardboard about the size of a playing card. Mark it like one of the cards in the top drawing above. You can make spots, stars, rabbits, or any design you wish. By carefully placing your fingers as you turn the card, you make it look as if the card had four different patterns.

PAPER MONEY

Show your friends both sides of a page from a newspaper. Fold the paper and turn it upside down. Out slides a penny. The secret lies in the newspaper. From a similar page of the paper (classified pages work best), cut a patch a little bigger than a penny. Paste or tape the patch to make an invisible pocket. Slip a penny into the pocket. When you perform the trick, show both sides of the page, then fold it so the pocket is hidden.

VANISHING COIN

Hold a coin as shown (below, figure 1). Pretend to take the coin with your right hand (2). While the fingers of your right hand hide the coin, let it fall into your left palm (3). Show your right hand as if the coin had vanished (4).

While the audience watches your empty right hand, quickly drop the coin into your pocket.

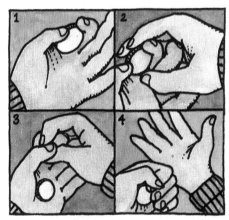

Now Get This Straight!

Bobby Taylor is having a friend over to study. His room is a mess (picture A), so Bobby decides to clean it up. That's his straightened room in picture B.

Bobby put a lot of things away. He repaired some and returned others to their proper parts of the house or to their owners. Your job: Figure out what is missing, what has been moved, and what has been repaired.

Deck your windows this holiday season, or anytime, with "stained-glass" cookies you make yourself.

COOKIE ORNAMENTS

"You can hang them in a window, put them on your tree, or give them to friends," says Paul Brunell. On these pages, Paul, 10, and his friend Nanine Rogers, 12, both from Washington, D. C., show you how to make "stained-glass" cookies. Ask an adult if it's all right to use the stove. Then get out the items listed in the box at right and follow these steps.

1 MEASURE THE INGREDIENTS. *Paul watches Nanine pour out the flour. After you have the right amount of each item, mash the margarine, sugar, and honey together in a bowl. Then stir in the water and mix until smooth.*

1/2 cup soft margarine
1 cup packed brown sugar
1/3 cup honey
1/4 cup water
1/2 teaspoon salt
1/2 teaspoon baking soda
3 cups sifted all-purpose
  flour
Bright-colored Lifesavers
  or lollipops
Large bowl
Wooden spoon
Measuring cups and
  spoons
Aluminum foil
Wax paper
Cookie sheets
4 or 5 small plastic bags

2 MIX THE DOUGH. *After stirring together the salt, baking soda, and flour, add them to the sugar mixture a little at a time. Paul and Nanine stir the ingredients with a large spoon. "The dough was very thick at first," Paul said.*

3 KNEAD...THEN CHILL. *Paul softens the dough by kneading it. "Just twist the dough around with your hands. It's fun because it feels squishy," explained Nanine. If you have trouble softening your dough, add a few drops of water and* knead it some more. Once the dough feels like soft clay, put it back in the bowl and chill it in the freezer for at least ten minutes or until it is firm enough to handle. Then, turn on the oven and set the temperature at 325 degrees.

6 PREPARE THE STAINED "GLASS." *Your cookie designs must bake for 5 to 8 minutes in a heated oven. While the cookies are baking, unwrap your candy. "Transparent Lifesavers or lollipops work well, or any other colored candy you can see through," said Nanine. Sort the* candy by color. Put each color into a plastic bag. "You have to keep the colors separate," Paul warned. "Only one color goes into each bag. Otherwise, the colors will run into each other when you bake them. Then you'll have muddy-looking windows."

7 CRACK THE CANDY. *Paul hits a bag of candy with a wooden spoon. "Give it medium-hard whacks," he said. The pieces should be small and thin, but still big enough to pick up. Put the candy into the refrigerator until you're ready to use it.*

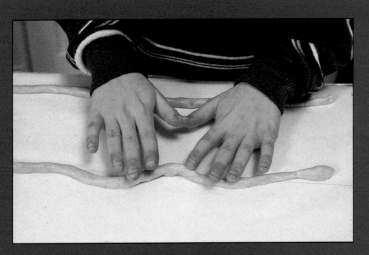

4 ROLL THE DOUGH INTO STRIPS. *Spread wax paper on the table. Pinch off a small ball of dough and put it on the paper. Roll it into a long, thin, rounded strip. Repeat until you have enough strips for several cookies.*

5 OUTLINE A DESIGN. *On a small piece of wax paper, shape the dough strips into a bird, bell, or whatever you like. Join the strips by pressing the ends together. Put a loop at the top for hanging. Cover a cookie sheet with foil. Carefully turn over the wax paper with the design onto the cookie sheet. Then peel away the wax paper, leaving the design on the foil. Put several designs on the foil. Allow plenty of space between them. Then put them in the oven.*

8 FILL THE WINDOWS. *Be sure to let the cookie sheet cool before you do this, so you won't burn your fingers. Then make the colored windows in your cookie shapes. Fill each outline with a thin, even layer of candy pieces. Use one color for each window. Now turn the candy pieces into "glass." Put your color-filled cookies back in the oven. Bake them until the candy melts and begins to bubble. This takes from 5 to 8 minutes. Baking time varies with the size and shape of the cookies. Watch them to make sure they don't burn!*

9 HANG AND ENJOY! *Nanine takes the hot cookies from the oven. After they have cooled and hardened, she'll peel them off the cookie sheet and pull off any foil that sticks to them. She and Paul will put string in the loops and hang them up for all to admire.*

Lunch-box Travel Kit

Going on a trip? If you plan ahead, the trip can be almost as much fun as reaching your destination. Just take along your own travel kit filled with interesting things to do.

Begin with a discarded lunch box. If the lunch box has patterns on it, you may want to cover it with unpatterned Con-Tact paper. That will give you a good surface for writing, drawing, or playing games. You can decorate the sides of the box with souvenir decals of places you visit.

Now select items to put inside the kit. You'll find some ideas on this page. Add anything else you like. On the opposite page are some games to play as you travel.

A small, lined spiral pad and pencil for writing a journal

Tiny game books (you can buy them at the grocery store)

An unlined pad of paper and colored pencils for drawing memorable sights

Sealable plastic bags to store items you pick up

A deck of cards

Crossword puzzles saved from newspapers

Plain postcards to color and send to friends

A set of magnetic checkers

A copy of the same road map the driver is using

A yard of string for making a cat's cradle

SUE LEVIN

COLOR COUNT

Red . . . blue . . . yellow . . . green. Cars come in a rainbow of colors. What's the favorite car color in the part of the country you're traveling through? Ask each person in your car to make a guess. Then run a survey to find out who's correct.
1) Write down the colors of the first 100 cars you pass and add the totals.
2) Assign each rider a color, starting with the highest total.
3) Set a time limit — 15 minutes in heavy traffic, more in light traffic. During that time, riders count only cars of their assigned color.
4) When time is up, total the scores. Did anyone guess the right color?

CAR GAMES

COUNTDOWN

Play this game during an extra-long car trip. Look for a license tag that begins with 9. Then try to spot other tags that begin with 8, 7, and so on, down to 1. For a more challenging game, find a tag that contains the letter Z. Then work back through the alphabet to A.

LADYBUG

If being in a car begins to bug you, try this counting game. Look for the numbers one through seven on street signs, billboards, or anywhere else. There's a catch: Each number must stand alone, and only the first player to see it may claim it. That player then draws part of a ladybug on a sheet of paper. The first player to finish the drawing wins.

1 - body   5 - left legs
2 - head   6 - right legs
3 - eyes   7 - spots
4 - antennae

Mix and Match

DANDELION

SUNFLOWER

GHOST ORCHID

GIANT BLAZING STAR

BLEEDING HEART

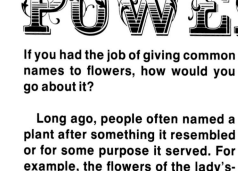

HAREBELL

QUEEN ANNE'S LACE

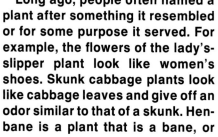

If you had the job of giving common names to flowers, how would you go about it?

Long ago, people often named a plant after something it resembled or for some purpose it served. For example, the flowers of the lady's-slipper plant look like women's shoes. Skunk cabbage plants look like cabbage leaves and give off an odor similar to that of a skunk. Henbane is a plant that is a bane, or

BUTTERFLY PEA

FLAME AZALEA

INDIAN PAINTBRUSH

poison, to chickens. Colic-root is a plant that people believed cured an ailment known as the colic.

Directions

On the left side of this page are some familiar things that people may have thought of when they looked at certain flowers. Beneath them are the actual flower names. Make a list from 1 to 10. Using the pictures as clues, see if you can match each flower on this page with its name.

TENT PARTY

Here's a super idea for a birthday party. Hold a sleep-out right in your own backyard. If you don't own a tent, make one. Ask an adult for an old tarp, a plastic drop cloth, and a clothesline. Find a level spot. Lay the drop cloth on the ground between two poles or between two trees. Stretch the clothesline between the poles or trees and drape the tarp over it. Anchor the sides of the tarp with rocks or with logs.

To turn your sleep-out into a party, invite enough friends to fill several tents. Then try some of the activities and games on these and the next pages.

FLASHLIGHT MORSE CODE

Have a message for a friend in another tent? Use the code that shortwave radio operators use. It's called the International Morse code, and it consists of a series of long and short blinker signals (right) or sounds. Send your messages by turning a flashlight on and off, as Chris Parsley, 12, of Barnesville, Maryland, is doing (left). He and A.J. Thompson, 11, of nearby Dickerson, are camping in a friend's yard.

MORSE CODE

A	B	C	D	E	F	G
H	I	J	K	L	M	N
O	P	Q	R	S	T	U
V	W	X	Y	Z

NUMERALS

1	2	3	4
5	6	7	8
9	0

PUNCTUATION

Period   Comma   Semicolon   Question Mark

HAND SHADOWS

Try your hands at this after-dark artwork. Shine your flashlight against the side of the tent. Put your hands between the tent and the light and try to make these animals.

BIRD IN FLIGHT

Raise your hands and cross them in front of you with the fingers together. Then link your thumbs. If you wave your fingers, you can make the bird fly.

BLACK SWAN

Raise your arm and curve your hand to make a swan's neck and head. With the fingers of your other hand, form the feathers on its wing.

ELEPHANT

Stretch out your left hand with the two middle fingers curved down and the other two fingers straight out. Drop your thumb slightly. This forms an elephant's tusks, trunk, and mouth. Curve your right hand and rest it on top of your left hand to make the elephant's head.

WHAT WAS THAT?

If you have a lot of friends at your sleep-out, here's a game that eight — or even more — people can play in the evening. Before starting, gather these items: a paper and a pencil for each player and 10 to 16 small objects, such as coins, crayons, paper clips, safety pins, pencils, and pebbles.

Appoint a scorekeeper. Give out the paper and pencils to the other players and have them sit in a circle with their hands behind their backs.

To start the game, the scorekeeper places one of the collected objects in the hands of one player without letting anyone in the group see it. That player passes it to the next player. The second player passes it to the third, and so on around the circle.

As soon as the first player's hands are empty, the scorekeeper fills them with the next object. As the object finishes its path around the circle, the scorekeeper collects it again.

When all of the objects have traveled around the circle, each player must quickly list all of the objects and the order in which they were passed.

The scorekeeper reads the correct list as the players X out their wrong answers. The player with the most correct answers wins.

GHOSTLY TALES

At night, campers often sit in the dark and whisper scary things. Here are some eerie ghost stories you can tell. Remember: A ghost story is only as good as the person telling it, so tell your story in as ghostly a voice as possible.

DARK, DARK, DARK

The night was dark, dark, dark. I was walking along a dark, dark road, and I came to a dark, dark house. I knocked on the dark, dark door.

NOBODY ANSWERED

(Make your voice quieter:) So I went in through the dark, dark door into a dark, dark hall. "Hello!" I said.

NOBODY ANSWERED

(Whisper:) So I went up the dark, dark stairs, and I went into a dark, dark room. Over in the dark, dark corner, I saw a dark, dark chest. So I opened it—and out jumped—a dark, dark . . .

(Jump up and shout:) GHOST!

PHANTOM HITCHHIKER

For this ghost story, you'll need to supply the name of an adult woman to fill in the ***'s.

One night when it was raining and very dark, *** was riding home in her car. As she stopped at a railroad crossing, she saw a young girl standing by the road. The girl's face was pale, and her clothing was dripping wet. *** asked the girl where she was going, and she gave *** an address that was directly on her

way home. So *** offered her a ride.

Feeling a strange coldness about the girl, *** loaned her a jacket. When they reached the girl's home, *** dropped her off and said she'd stop by for the jacket the next day.

The next morning, she returned. An older woman answered the door. "I came for the jacket that I lent your daughter last night," she explained.

"But that's impossible," the old woman said. "My daughter Mary was killed by a train three years ago last night."

A week later, *** passed a cemetery. Haunted by the girl, she turned in. As she stopped by a tombstone, a shock went through her. There on the tombstone was the name of her passenger. Folded at its foot was her jacket.

Let's Observe Passover

At the feast of Passover, Jews celebrate a joyous event in the history of their ancestors, the Hebrews: being "passed over" when the angel of death slaughtered the firstborn child in other homes, escaping from slavery under an Egyptian pharaoh, and journeying safely to freedom.

WORD COUNT

A highlight of Passover is a family feast called the seder (SAY-der). During the seder, family members use symbolic objects to remind them of important events during the escape from Egypt. One symbol is a lamb shankbone. Blood from a sacrificed lamb saved the Hebrews from the slaughter of the firstborn. Another is matzo, a cracker-shaped bread. It represents the hastily prepared bread the Hebrews took with them as they fled. At the seder, a matzo called the afikoman serves as the traditional dessert.

See how many words you can make from the letters of each one of these three words: Passover, shankbone, and afikoman. Don't use any letter more times than it appears in a word.

NUTTY RACE

The seder table usually includes a bowl of nuts. Nuts were among the wild foods that kept the Hebrews alive on their journey. Try this seder game. Give each player an empty bowl, some nuts, and two pencils. See who can be the first to move six nuts from the table into the bowl using the pencils.

PASSOVER RIDDLES

What is flat and picks up pins?
When is a piece of wood like Pharaoh?

FRUITFUL JOURNEY

At seder, play this alphabet game between courses of the dinner. The leader begins putting the afikoman on his or her shoulder. The player to that player's right asks, "Who are you? Where are you from? Where are you going? What will you take on your journey?"

The leader answers: "My name is (leader's name). I'm leaving Egypt to be free in Israel. I'm taking *apples* with me." The next player takes the afikoman and answers the questions in the same way—adding a food beginning with the next letter of the alphabet. For example, "I'm taking *apples* and *bananas*."

Play continues clockwise, with each player repeating the list and adding a new food. Whoever forgets an item must drop out. Continue until only one player remains.

If you run out of conversation at the dinner table some evening, test your family's knowledge of American history with these statements. Are they true or false? The answers are in the answer pages, but for the whole story, look up each name in an encyclopedia.

1) General Robert E. Lee was wearing a coonskin cap when he was killed during the Battle of the Alamo.

2) The teddy bear was named after President Theodore Roosevelt.

3) Astronaut Sally Ride was the first woman to walk on the moon.

4) Martin Luther King was President of the United States from 1956 until 1960.

5) Benjamin Franklin flew a kite with a metal key attached to prove that lightning is electricity.

6) The electric light bulb was invented by Alexander Graham Bell.

7) While he was president, George Washington, his wife, Martha, and their 13 children lived in the White House.

8) Charles Lindbergh made the first solo airplane flight around the world.

9) A nurse named Betsy Ross wrote the words to "The Star-Spangled Banner" in 1778, during the Revolutionary War.

10) Amelia Earhart was the first woman to sail alone across the Atlantic Ocean.

11) Thomas Jefferson and John Adams, both U. S. Presidents and signers of the Declaration of Independence, died on the same day — July 4, 1826.

12) Thomas Edison invented the phonograph — in spite of being almost totally deaf.

FUN-DAY REBUS

Looking for a purr-fect spot for your family to spend a spare afternoon or weekend? There's a whale of an idea right on this page. It's hidden above, in the combination of words, pictures, and symbols called a rebus.

After you have figured out the message, try it. Then try drawing a rebus of your own. First, write out your message. Then substitute pictures for some words or parts of words. Add or subtract letters when necessary, as the author of this rebus has done. Hint: In a rebus, the way a word sounds is more important than the way it's spelled.

With Dough

When most people think of dough, they think of cookies and other holiday treats that are good to eat. But there's a special kind of dough that you wouldn't want to eat because it doesn't taste good. People use it to make colorful holiday decorations and gifts. To learn how, turn the page.

Holiday Dough

Ingredients

4 cups of flour
1 cup of salt
1¹/₄ cups of water
(sometimes more)

Mix the flour and salt thoroughly in a big bowl. Add water. Stir the mixture until it forms a sticky mass. When the mixture becomes too stiff to stir, work it with your hands. This is called kneading.

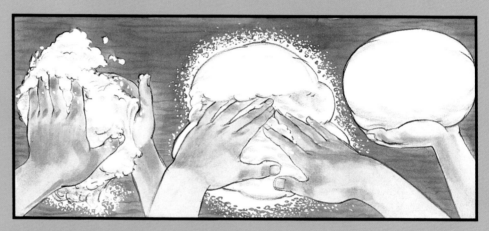

Knead the dough on a breadboard or on a cutting board. To keep the dough from sticking to the board, sprinkle both with flour. Roll the dough into a ball. Flatten the ball with the heels of your hands. Continue rolling and flattening for about ten minutes. The dough should feel like soft modeling clay.

Shape the dough into figures. Use a toothpick to add features to the faces and details to the clothes. If you roll out the dough so that it is about half an inch thick, you can cut flat designs with a cookie cutter. You can shape a puppet on your finger.

Bake thick shapes on an ungreased cookie sheet for about an hour at 350 degrees. Bake thin shapes for about half an hour at the same temperature. Remember to ask an adult's permission to use the oven. Using pot holders, remove the cookie sheet from the oven and let the figures cool for an hour.

Decorate the figures. Tempera or poster paints work best for dough figures. Let the paint dry for a few hours. If you want to give your ornaments a shiny finish, brush them with clear nail polish. Now your creations are complete. On the next page, you'll see some ideas for gifts you can make.

Things to Make

Clothespin characters made with dough can help decorate your house. Use all-wood clothespins. Cover the top of each one with a thick layer of dough, then shape the dough. Slip the clothespins over the rim of a deep baking pan and bake the figures for one hour at 350 degrees. Let them cool, then paint them. Clip the figures on a Christmas tree or on a lamp shade.

Jewelry can be made from dough. To make a necklace, leave a small hole in a dough figure. When you have baked and painted the figure, slip a string or a chain through the hole. To make a pin, press a safety pin into the back of a figure before baking it.

Frame a favorite snapshot. Press the picture into a block of dough and mold a frame around it. Bake the frame with the picture inside. Make sure the picture doesn't touch the cookie sheet. For a larger picture, mold dough into the shape of a frame. Bake just the frame, then decorate it. Glue the edges of the picture onto the underside of the frame.

Ornaments should be lightweight, so they won't pull down the branches of a Christmas tree. To make hanging easy, leave a hole in the top of each ornament for a string. You also can press a paper clip or an ornament hanger into the dough figure before baking it.

Magnets can be fun. Design a figure from dough. Before you bake it, press a small, strong bar magnet into the bottom. Make sure that one surface of the magnet has no dough on it. When you have baked and painted the figure, you can put it on your refrigerator to hold messages. You can also do tricks with the figure. Put it on a piece of cardboard or on a magazine. Use another magnet underneath to make your dough figure move.

Brain Check

Testing . . . testing . . . this is a brain check. Is yours working today? It is? Then focus your mental energy on these puzzles. If you solve them all, go to the head of the class.

COLOR MIX-UP

After some art students finished painting a mural on the art room wall, they played a joke on the rest of the class. They switched the caps on the red, pink, purple, green and yellow paint jars they had used, so each jar had a cap of a different color. They left these clues on the blackboard.
1) The red paint is next to the jar with the purple cap.
2) The pink and purple paints are not next to each other.
3) One jar stands between the green and red paints.
4) The yellow paint is second from the left.

Can you figure out what color paint is in each jar in the box?

SOCK SORT

Pop! Your bedroom light just blew out, and you're late for a party. You open your sock drawer knowing it contains 10 white socks and 20 red socks. How many socks would you have to pull out to make a matching pair?

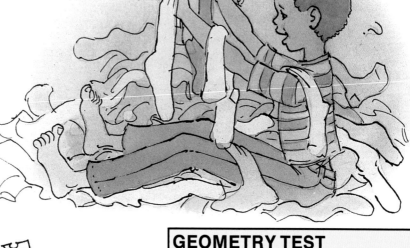

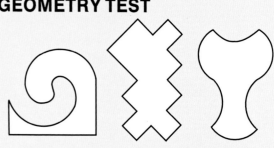

STAMP COUNT

Don't let this sticky little question lick you. If there are 12 one-cent stamps in a dozen, how many 22-cent stamps are there in a dozen?

GEOMETRY TEST

You'll need a piece of tracing paper to try this teaser. Trace the four shapes shown here. Now draw a line on each one that cuts it into two identical halves. The line may be straight, curved, or angled.

String a popcorn chain...

...to trim a tree or a window. You'll need popped corn, fresh cranberries, white thread, a needle, and a thimble.

Cut a piece of thread about as long as a yardstick. Push one end through the needle. In the other end, tie several knots in one place to make one *big* knot. Push the needle through a piece of popcorn. Wear a thimble to protect your finger. Move the popcorn along  the thread until it reaches the knot.

Alternate a kernel of popcorn with a cranberry, or try different patterns. When you reach the end of the thread, tie another big knot at the other end to complete your string.

After the holidays are over, you can hang your decoration outside for the birds to eat.

What can you do with popcorn?

MUNCH IT *or use it to make trimmings and treats for the holidays. The munchers are Julie Shea, 12, of Great Falls, Virginia, and Adam Green, 12, of Washington, D. C. The directions for trimmings and treats are on this page.*

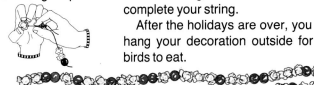

Make popcorn balls...

...to share with your friends. You'll need 2 tablespoons of unpopped corn, salt, 35 vanilla caramels, and $2\frac{1}{2}$ tablespoons of water.

Pop the corn according to the directions on the package. Put it in a large bowl and add a little salt.

Ask an adult to help you with the rest. Unwrap the caramels and put them in a saucepan with the water. Turn the heat on low. Stir the mixture constantly until all of the candy melts.

When the caramel mixture is thick and smooth, pour it over the popcorn. Stir the popcorn quickly until the caramel covers all of it.

As soon as the caramel-covered corn is cool enough to handle, spoon some of it out of the bowl. Press it into balls the size of apples. Let them harden overnight. Then wrap them in thin plastic, add ribbon, and give them to friends.

Trim a popcorn tree...

...to put on the holiday table. *For the tree,* you'll need popped corn, straight pins, a Styrofoam cone 8 inches tall, and an empty thread spool. *For the candy coating,* you'll need 1 cup of powdered sugar, 1/3 cup of boiling water, 3 drops of green food coloring, a large bowl, and a spoon.

Pin a row of popped corn around the bottom edge of the cone. The kernels should touch. Push each pin in firmly. For large kernels, you may need two pins. Continue making rows until

you have covered the cone. Fill in any bare spots with small kernels.

Measure the sugar into a bowl. Add the boiling water and food coloring. Stir until the sugar disappears.

Hold the cone upside down over the bowl. Tilt the cone and spoon the sugar solution over it. Some will drip into the bowl. Keep spooning the solution over the tree until all the kernels are covered and the tree is a shade of green you like. Let the tree dry for

about two days. The popcorn will shrink. Pin on gumdrops to fill the bare spots. Glue a spool to the base of the cone to form a trunk. Stand your tree on a table and admire it, but don't eat it!

Pick a puzzle

FOLLOW THIS TRAIL

This drawing has only one line
The arrow points to one end
Where is the other end?

QUARTER TURNS

Pretend you have a quarter. Imagine you are rolling it around the three quarters above. As it rolls, it always touches at least one of the three coins. How many complete turns will the quarter make before it returns to its starting place?

MONEY GAME

Imagine you have a number of United States coins in your pocket. (You have no dollars.) What is the largest amount of money you can have without being able to make exact change for a dollar, a half dollar, a quarter, a dime, or a nickel? Hint: To make change for a nickel you must have five pennies. So you have only four pennies in your pocket. Now figure out what other coins you have.

BOO!

When ghosts and goblins are about to make their yearly visit, plan a spooky party for your friends.

Matthew Russell, 11, of Westtown, Pennsylvania, has turned himself into a ghoul with some things he found in the kitchen. For his "mask," he smeared his face with honey and pressed on cornmeal and bran. An orange peel forms fangs. Eyebrow pencil makes dark eyebrows.

On the next pages, Matthew and Kirsten Earl, 10, of Medford, New Jersey, will show you ways to spook up your own haunted home.

PIPE-CLEANER SPIDER

Things you will need to make one spider: (found at hobby shops)
2 black pipe cleaners, 12 inches long
2 plastic doll eyes
1 black pom-pom

Cut each pipe cleaner in half. Put all four pieces side by side and twist them together at the middle. Hold them at the twist with one hand while you gently bend the pipe cleaners into eight spider legs. Glue the pom-pom to the twist at the center of the legs. Glue the two eyes to the pom-pom.

SMALL GHOSTS

Things you will need:
Small round or oval balloons
White wrapping tissue (20 inches on a side or larger)
Rubber bands
String
Black felt-tip marker

1) Blow up several balloons and knot them at the neck. (You may want to ask an adult to help.)
2) Place each balloon in the center of a sheet of tissue paper. Gather the paper around the balloon and secure it with a rubber band.
3) Draw a scary face on each ghost.
4) Hang each ghost up by tying a string to the rubber band.

Putting together some Halloween fun, Matthew and Kirsten add details to little white ghosts (below), twist fuzzy black spiders (left), and glue a glow-in-the-dark spiderweb (right).

STRING-AND-GLUE SPIDERWEBS

Things you will need:
Yardstick
Ball of thick white yarn
White household glue
Water
Old plastic bowl or other container
Paintbrushes
Scissors
Glow-in-the-dark paint
Waxed paper

STEPS:
1) Spread waxed paper over your work surface.
2) For each web, cut 3 pieces of yarn 2 feet long, and one piece 6 feet long.
3) In the bowl, mix 1 tablespoon of glue with 1 tablespoon of water.
4) Soak the shorter pieces of yarn in the glue mixture and arrange them like spokes on the waxed paper.
5) Soak the longer piece of yarn in the glue mixture and spiral it out from the center of the spokes in a web pattern.
6) Let the web dry. Paint it with the glow-in-the-dark paint.
7) After the paint dries, turn the paper over and carefully peel it off the web.
8) Hang the web anywhere you like.

BUILD A SPOOK HOUSE

If you want to put some extra chills into Halloween, build your own spook house and invite your friends in for a scare. You'll need some large cardboard boxes. A supermarket or a department or appliance store may have extra ones.

Open the ends of the boxes and tape them together to form a zigzag tunnel. Paint the insides of the boxes with black poster paint. Cut holes shaped like pairs of animal eyes in the sides of the tunnel and cover them with orange tissue paper so light can enter. Decorate the tunnel with witches, ghosts, and spiderwebs.

To add scare appeal, arrange cold, cooked spaghetti strings along the sides of the tunnel, where visitors are most apt to touch them. Play whispering voices and other sound effects that you have tape-recorded. Add any eerie ideas of your own.

LONELY GHOST

How sly a ghost are you? This game will challenge your ghostly powers of winking. Four to 53 people can play. All you need is a pack of playing cards.

TO START: The players form a circle. One player serves as the dealer. The dealer takes enough cards from the deck to equal the number of players. One of the cards must be a joker. The dealer shuffles the cards taken from the deck and gives every player one, face down. Each player looks at the card without letting anyone else see it. Whoever gets the joker is the lonely ghost.

OBJECT: The lonely ghost tries to make ghosts of other players by winking at them without being seen by anyone except the person being winked at. If the lonely ghost makes ghosts of all the other players, the lonely ghost wins the game. But if a player catches the lonely ghost winking at someone else, that player wins the game.

TO PLAY: Only the lonely ghost is allowed to wink. A player who gets a ghostly wink must count to five silently, then say, "You got me." That player becomes a ghost and is out of the game. Anyone who thinks he or she sees the lonely ghost wink, can ask, "Are you the lonely ghost?" If the answer is "yes," the lonely ghost must say so. If the answer is "no," the person who asked the question becomes a ghost and is out of the game. The game goes on until the lonely ghost is found, or until all the players become ghosts.

HINT: Fast winkers are hard to catch. To keep from being caught, practice winking at yourself in a mirror.

BAT-AND-WITCH MOBILE

Things you'll need:
Tracing paper
Pencil
Carbon paper
Black construction paper
Brown and black tissue paper
Transparent tape
Household glue
Scissors
Straws
Needle and thread

Steps: Put a sheet of tracing paper over the bat drawing on page 61 and trace it, including the dotted-line wings.

Transfer the traced drawing onto construction paper this way:
1) Place black construction paper on a smooth table.
2) On top of that, lay a sheet of carbon paper, with the shiny carbon side down.
3) Tape the corners of the carbon paper to the construction paper.
4) Place your tracing of the bat on the construction paper and trace only the solid lines. Don't trace the dotted lines.
5) Cut out the bat.

Glue the bat onto brown tissue paper and carefully draw in the dotted-line wings freehand. If you have trouble, transfer the dotted-line wings from your tracing the same way you transferred the bat to the construction paper. Cut out the entire bat from the tissue paper.

Make a witch following steps 1-5 above. Then cut out a black tissue cape and glue it to the witch's back.

For each mobile, you'll need at least three figures — all bats, all witches, or a combination of the two.

Now assemble your mobile. Build a frame by pushing a needle and knotted thread through one end of a straw and into the center of a second straw. Leave about 10 inches of thread between the two straws. Cut the thread and knot it so the thread stays in place.

Pull a separate thread through the head of a bat or through the hat of a witch and draw the thread through one of the three straw ends remaining. Knot the end of the thread. Leave from 8 to 12 inches of thread between the bat or witch and the straw. Attach the other two figures to the other straw ends in the same way.

Complete the mobile this way: Loop a thread over the center of the first straw and knot its ends together. This loop is the hanger. To balance the mobile, slide the loop left or right, as Kirsten does, until the mobile hangs straight. Then tape the loop in place.

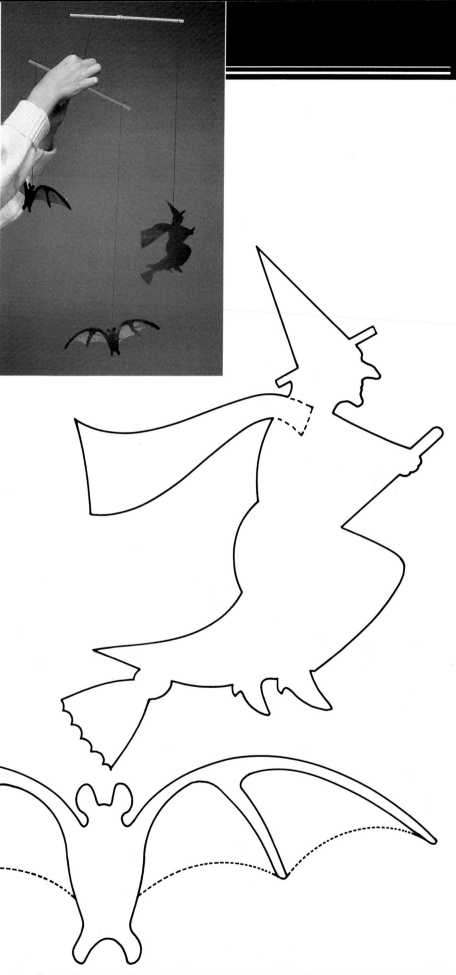

After gluing a bat onto brown tissue paper and drawing in wings, Matthew carefully trims away the extra tissue.

ROAD SIGNS

1

What can they tell you?

The next time you're out riding in a car, take a careful look at the signs along the road. These signs give people important information in words, in pictures, or in combinations of both.

Some, such as no-passing signs, tell drivers not to do certain things. Other signs warn drivers to be on guard for various things — such as turtles or other animals crossing the road. Some signs let drivers know that services or attractions — such as gas stations or parks — are nearby.

The shape of a sign often gives a clue to its meaning. Certain shapes mean the same thing throughout the United States. For example, a triangle with three equal sides and with the point down means "yield." When you see an eight-sided sign, it means "stop." A diamond-shaped sign warns drivers to watch out for possible dangers on or near the road. In other countries, these shapes may mean different things.

More and more, pictures are used on signs instead of words. Drivers often have very little time to read a sign and grasp its message. Traffic experts say drivers can understand pictures faster than they can understand words. To see how well you can read road-sign pictures, play the game below.

5

How many can you match?

The road signs on the right come from all over the world. Look at them carefully. Then try to match each sign with a description and location from the list below. Make a list from 1 to 12.

Then select your choice from the columns below and write the letter beside the corresponding number. If you get crossed up, check the answers on page 102.

A. *Cow crossing, Turkey*

B. *Hippopotamus crossing, Zambia*

C. *Watch out for thieves, Denmark*

D. *Moose crossing, Finland*

E. *Pedestrian crossing, Switzerland*

F. *Turtle crossing, Connecticut*

G. *Watch for horse-drawn carts, Ohio*

H. *Elephant crossing, Zambia*

I. *Fire truck crossing, West Virginia*

J. *Goose crossing, Maryland*

K. *Horse and rider crossing, Maryland*

L. *Deer crossing, Virginia*

9

2

3

4

6

7

Pas på tyven

8

10

11

12

Kwanzaa

Hanukkah...Christmas...Kwanzaa. Each of these holidays has a special meaning for certain groups of people. Kwanzaa (KWAHN-zah) is a celebration for black American families. It's a time to remember their heritage, to look back on their good fortune during the past year, and to express their hopes for the year to come.

Kwanzaa began in 1966. The word comes from an African language called Swahili. Kwanzaa stands for "first" in the phrase "first fruits."

Kwanzaa lasts for seven days, from December 26 to January 1. Like other important holidays, it has certain symbols that add meaning to it.

On these and the next pages, you'll find out how to make and use some Kwanzaa symbols. You will also discover what each one means.

BOWL

Kwanzaa celebrations usually include a colorful bowl filled with *mazao* (muh-ZOW)—fresh fruits, vegetables, and nuts. These represent the fruits of the harvest. The bowl also may contain *zawadi* (zah-WAH-dee)—meaningful objects or handmade gifts for the children of the family. To make a papier-mâché bowl, collect these items.

2 bowls	Shortening
Newspapers	Scissors
Flour	Water
Paints	Paintbrush

Now, follow these steps.

1) Cut the newspaper into strips about an inch wide.

2) Grease the inside of one of the bowls with shortening.

3) In the other bowl, mix one cup of flour and 2/3 cup of water. Stir until the mixture is about as thick as pancake batter.

4) Slide a strip of newspaper through the paste mixture. Then pull it gently through your fingers to wipe off the excess glue. Lay the strip on the inside surface of the greased bowl as a liner.

5) Repeat step 4 with the other newspaper strips, crisscrossing them until you have covered the inside of the bowl with three layers.

6) Let the strips dry completely.

7) Carefully trim the extra paper from the edges of the bowl to make an even rim. Then gently lift the papier-mâché bowl out of the real bowl.

8) Paint your papier-mâché bowl a bright color. Add designs if you like.

9) After the paint has dried, protect the bowl with a thin coating of equal parts white glue and water.

At the Anacostia Neighborhood Museum, in Washington, D.C., young artists (above) hold some of the symbols a family uses to observe Kwanzaa. From the left, the artists are (front row) Jó Shonda Reece, 12, of Oxon Hill, Maryland, and Octavia Anderson, 12, Lisa Miller, 14, Keisha Roaché, 11, (back row) Michael Washington, 15, Dartanyan Edmonds, 15, Marc Jackson, 14, and Stephani McDow, 10, all of Washington. At left, Keisha and Stephani build a papier-mâché bowl.

MISHUMAA SABA

On each day during Kwanzaa, families light a candle and think about one of seven different ideals to live by. The seven candles of Kwanzaa are called the *mishumaa saba* (mee-SHOO-mah SAH-bah).

Make a mishumaa and candleholder, or *kinara* (kee-NAR-ah) out of construction paper and cardboard egg cartons. You'll need two cartons.

Cut one carton so it has only two pairs of egg compartments. Set the end compartments of the whole egg carton into the end compartments of the cut carton so they lock together. Close the lids and tape all around the edges. Now you should have what looks like a 14-egg carton. Turn the carton over and cut slits in the bottoms of one row of egg compartments to hold the candles.

To make the candles, cut strips of paper 3 inches wide and 8 inches long. Curve the strips into cylinders and tape the edges together. Make one black, three green, and three red candles. These colors symbolize black people, youth and the future, and struggle.

"Lighting" a candle, Jó Shonda tapes on a cardboard flame.

Lisa and Marc weave strips of newspaper into a mat.

MKEKA

The *mkeka* (mm-KAY-kah), a woven mat, stands for the foundation of the traditions of black Americans. All the other symbols of Kwanzaa rest on the mkeka. You can make a newspaper mkeka.

First make a frame. Find a single sheet of newspaper (or cut a double sheet in half.) Starting at a shorter end, fold over 2 inches of the newspaper and continue folding until you have a flat roll. Unroll half of the newspaper and, from the unrolled end, roll the paper toward the center. You should have a V-shaped roll. Roll three other sheets the same way.

Interlock the corners of three of the strips at right angles so they form three sides of a frame. Staple them at the corners. Lay the frame on a table with the open end facing you.

Fold other sheets of newspaper into 2-inch strips and lay them edge to edge inside the slot of the middle frame section. Staple them in place.

Then weave other strips across the frame until you have filled it. Staple the strips into the side frame pieces.

Complete your mat by adding and stapling the bottom section of the frame in place.

Now paint your mat with acrylic or poster paint. Red, green, and black are the traditional colors of Kwanzaa, but you may use other colors. After the paint has dried, you may add a thin coat of glue mixed with an equal amount of water to preserve your mkeka.

Protected by plastic, Dartanyan ties fabric for dyeing.

TIE-DYEING

Tie-dyed cloth is a tradition in many cultures. During Kwanzaa, it may serve as a tablecloth or a wall decoration. Tie-dyeing is *messy*. Don't do it where you can stain something valuable. Ask an adult's permission before you begin.

Things you'll need:
Powdered fabric dyes (from any grocery or drugstore)
Large pan or kettle
Mixing bowl for each color of dye
Rubber gloves
Rubber bands
Sheet of protective plastic
Whatever you want to tie-dye — 100 percent cotton cloth works best (wash new fabrics first)

Spread the plastic over the area where you'll work. Dampen whatever you are going to dye and wring it out. Now, follow these steps:

1) Heat a large pan of water.

2) Tie off sections of the material you want to dye with rubber bands. There are some tying ideas at left.

3) Wearing rubber gloves, fill one of the mixing bowls with hot water and stir in one color of dye, following the directions on the package.

4) Dip a tied-off area of cloth in the dye. If you want a light color, leave it in the dye for only a few minutes. If you want a darker color, leave it in the dye longer — up to 20 minutes. Colors will always look darker when the material is wet.

5) When the color is slightly darker than you want it, remove the article from the dye and gently squeeze out the water.

6) If you want to dye the article other colors, mix the dyes one at a time, repeating steps 3, 4, and 5 above.

7) When you have dyed all of the sections you want, rinse your material in cool water until the water runs clear. Then remove the rubber bands and rinse again until the water runs clear.

8) Hang the cloth in the shade to dry.

CIRCLE: Push up some fabric with your finger and wrap a rubber band tightly around its neck.

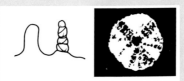

SUNBURST: Start this as you formed the circle. Then wrap another rubber band unevenly but tightly around the top.

STRIPES: Use a ruler and chalk to draw a series of parallel lines. Fold the fabric back and forth along the lines to form pleats. Then bind the pleated fabric with a rubber band.

DOUGHNUT: Push up a fabric section as you did for the circle. Then use your finger to push the top back through the neck. Wrap the neck with the rubber band.

SCAVENGER HUNT

Want to liven up a dull afternoon? Organize a scavenger hunt! A scavenger hunt is a race against the clock to collect all the objects on a list. You'll need enough players for two or more evenly matched teams. Provide each team with these items:

> **List of objects**
> **Paper**
> **Pencil**
> **Bag**

Make sure someone on each team has a watch. Before sending the teams off on their search, set a time limit. Forty-five minutes should be enough.

As the team finds each item, a team member crosses it off the list. The team that collects the most objects within the time limit — or returns first with the complete list — wins.

Here are some things you might want to put on your list. Add or subtract items, or substitute some of your own.

Berry
Three kinds of leaves
Something blue
Pure white rock
Aluminum can
Feather
Something that floats
Something square
Seed
Piece of tree bark
Two kinds of grass
Name of a tree you see
Something round
Acorn or nut
Pinecone
Clover leaf

Remind all players to avoid trespassing on private property.

WHAT IN THE WORLD KINDS OF JOBS ARE THESE?

How well do you know your way around the world of work? Test your knowledge here. The pictures below show tools used in six different jobs you can do. Can you guess what these jobs are? The clues will help you.

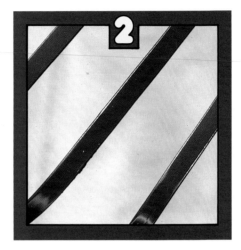

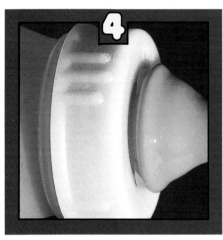
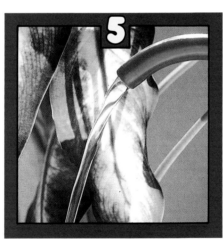

1 Exercise your right to make a profit by collaring the market on this. You may be embarking on a grrrreat career.

2 If you get a good grip on this and don't let things pile up on you, you can clean up financially. Success will be in the bag.

3 Use this to brighten a beetle, spruce up a Skyhawk, or put a gleam on a Gremlin—and you'll also build up your billfold.

4 This and a tin of talc are part of the formula for this trade. Use them promptly, or you'll receive some earsplitting complaints.

5 Don't count on showers to help you in this blooming business. You have to pour on the effort to reap financial rewards.

6 You must be a smart cookie to make dough in this business. Try not to do a half-baked job. Then people will say, "Well done."

WORKING FOR MONEY

School's out, your homework is done, and you have a lot of free time—but no money. Why not turn that free time into cash? There are many ways to earn spending money if you don't mind a little work.

JOBS GALORE

You'll find some kid-tested ideas in the pictures on these and the preceding page. There are hundreds more. You could put on a puppet show . . . recycle rubbish . . . build bird feeders . . . run errands for older neighbors . . . peddle plants . . . bake cakes . . . plan parties for tots . . . . Just make sure that what you decide to do is something you enjoy—something that still will be interesting to you after a week or two.

CAN YOU DO IT?

Once you make a job plan, think about these questions before you actually put it into action:
1) Are you ready to take on the responsibility of a job? Ask yourself—or a parent or a teacher—for an honest opinion. Once you agree to do something for someone, it's important that you actually do it. The one day you forget to water the plants or to walk the dog, for example, might result in dead plants or a ruined carpet—and a stained reputation.
2) Do you really know how to do the job? If you don't, find out. Ask a parent, a friend with experience, or even a professional, to show you the ropes.
3) Do you have enough time to do a thorough job?
4) Have you saved enough money to buy any equipment you might need to get started? A car-cleaning operation, for example, requires paper towels, sponges, soap, wax, glass cleaner, and other things. If you don't have enough cash to start your business, arrange a loan from a parent—or a brother or a sister. Just make sure you repay

the loan from your first earnings.
5) Do you have a substitute in case something unforeseen occurs? Hire one, if necessary.

WHERE TO START

There are many places to look for a job. Perhaps the first is right in your own home. Look around your house or apartment. What, other than your normal chores, needs doing? Are the windows dirty? Is the storeroom or the garage cluttered? Do the flowerbeds need weeding? Does the sidewalk need edging? Could the family car use a thorough cleaning inside and out? Think of things adults don't like—or don't have time—to do. Wait until your mom or dad has time to discuss your ideas, and then offer a deal. If it's reasonable, you'll get the job.

SPREADING THE WORD

You've decided what you want to do. Now, how do you get business? Advertise. Make an illustrated poster describing your service. Include your name, your address, your phone number (ask a parent's permission to list your phone number), the hours that you can work, and the cost of the service. Display your poster in areas where people know you. Ask permission to put your poster in store windows. Add it to the grocery-store bulletin board. Insert flyers in people's mailboxes or put them in plastic bags and hang them on doorknobs. Make calling cards and hand-deliver them to neighbors. Place an ad in your local newspaper.

MAKE A CONTRACT

After you have accepted a job, make sure both you and your employer know what's expected. Don't be afraid to ask questions. If you're going to pet-sit, for example, find out exactly what the pet eats and when. Find out the phone

number of the pet's veterinarian. Does the pet need any medicine? If the pet is a dog, when and where should you walk it? If it's an indoor animal, how often should you clean its cage or litter box? Make a list of what you have promised to do and ask the employer to read it. Agree on a fair price. If you don't know what to charge, ask experienced friends what their rates are and charge

Summer, winter, spring, or fall, there are always money-making jobs to be done — as these workers demonstrate.

the same — or less if you're a beginner on a difficult job. If you are going to work at homes when owners are away, write down a phone number to call in case of an emergency.

KEY TO SUCCESS

Do a good job. If you do, customers will call you back again and again. They'll think of you when other jobs come up. They'll tell their friends how responsible you are, and you'll soon have more jobs than you can accept. Don't fill all your free time with work, however. Leave some time for fun.

FORM A CO-OP

If you want to work and still have time to have fun with your friends, invite them to form a co-op. Together, you can organize a neighborhood dog wash or car wash, a housecleaning service, or a baby-sitting center. If you do go into business with other people, appoint one person to keep careful records of every penny each of you earns and spends. Make sure every member of the co-op gets a fair share of the profits.

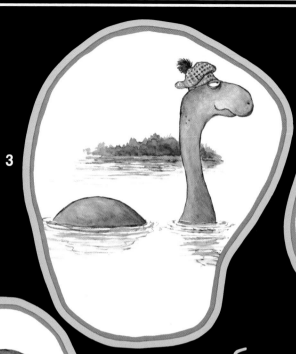

3

4

5

MONSTER MATCH

7

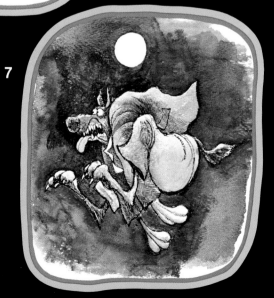

2

Monster names:
Loch Ness Monster
Cyclops
Sphinx
Harpy
Medusa
Abominable Snowman
Bigfoot
Troll
Werewolf

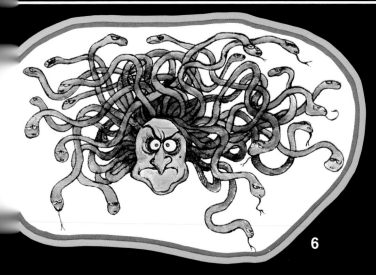

6

1

9

8

Do you recognize the monsters in these cartoons? You may have read about them in fairy tales and legends. A few have been in movies. Some people think one or two might really exist. How many of these monsters do you know by name? Match each picture with one of the clues below. Together, the picture and clue will help you guess the monster's name. Make a list from 1 to 9, and write in the name of each monster as you figure out the clues. If you get stumped, check the names below at left, or turn to the answer pages.

1 Folktales from Scandinavia tell about ugly creatures like this. They could be large or small, and they had magic powers. Most lived underground or in caves. A famous story from Norway tells about one that lived under a bridge.

2 Ancient Greeks and Romans wrote about this creature. They said it was half woman and half bird. It punished people for evil deeds by stealing their food and making unpleasant noises.

3 People still hunt for this monster in Scotland. The monster's name contains the name of a famous lake, where it is said to live.

4 This creature had the head of a person and the body of a lion. In ancient Egypt, people carved stone statues of it. One of the statues sits near the Nile.

5 Some people in North America think this furry brown monster tramps the woods and mountains of the West. They say they have seen its big footprints.

6 This woman had snakes all over her head. A Greek legend says that when people looked at her, they turned to stone.

7 When the moon is full, legends say, this creature grows fur and howls like a wolf. At sunrise, it changes into a man.

8 Some people say this white furry monster lives in the mountains of Asia. They believe it may be related to the mountain monster of North America.

9 In old Greek tales, this creature belonged to a race of giants who ate people. Each had only one eye—right in the middle of the forehead.

PRESENTS FOR PETS

For the holiday season, or for any special time, you can make a present for your pet. If you don't have a pet, make something for the wild birds to enjoy. Here are some gift ideas for your cat, dog, bird, or small, furry animal, such as a gerbil, a hamster, or a guinea pig.

SEW A MOUSE

You will need: Bright-colored felt material, tracing paper, a pencil, scissors, straight pins, thread, a needle, and catnip. You can buy catnip at pet or garden stores.

1 Trace the mouse and the ears shown below. Cut out the shapes you traced. They will be your patterns. Pin the mouse pattern to a piece of felt. Cut around the edge. Repeat with another piece of felt. You will have two identical mouse shapes. Make two felt ears the same way.

2 Cut about 20 inches of thread. Knot one end. Push the other end through the needle.

3 Put the mouse shapes together. Sew around the edges with stitches like those below. Leave an opening at the top. Fill the mouse with catnip. Sew up the opening and knot the thread. Attach the ears with harmless (nontoxic) white glue.

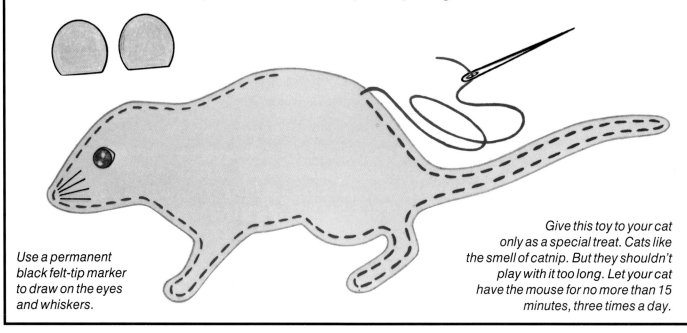

Use a permanent black felt-tip marker to draw on the eyes and whiskers.

Give this toy to your cat only as a special treat. Cats like the smell of catnip. But they shouldn't play with it too long. Let your cat have the mouse for no more than 15 minutes, three times a day.

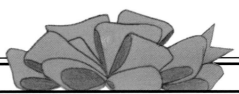

GROW SOME GREENS

You will need: Alfalfa or mung bean seeds, a quart glass jar with a large opening, an old nylon stocking, and a rubber band.

Put 2 tablespoons of seeds in a quart jar. Fill the jar half full of lukewarm water. Cover it with fabric from the stocking. Hold the stocking in place with the rubber band. Let the seeds soak for 24 hours.

Pour off the water. Rinse the seeds four times with cool water. Drain them completely. Replace the nylon. Lay the jar on its side. Cover it with a cloth. Don't cover the open end. Air that enters through the nylon helps your seeds sprout. Continue to rinse and drain the seeds at least once a day for three or four days.

When the alfalfa sprouts are about 1 inch long or when the mung bean sprouts are about 2 inches long, they are ready to feed to your hamster, gerbil, or guinea pig. You can save extra sprouts in the refrigerator, or eat them yourself. But don't keep them longer than a week because they may spoil.

TREAT THE BIRDS

You will need: birdseed, 1 egg, 1 tablespoon of honey, an egg carton, plastic food wrap (12 by 13 inches), 6 pieces of yarn (each 8 inches long), pointed scissors, 6 small metal bells.

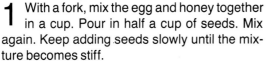

1 With a fork, mix the egg and honey together in a cup. Pour in half a cup of seeds. Mix again. Keep adding seeds slowly until the mixture becomes stiff.

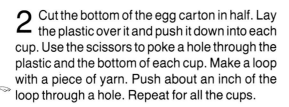

2 Cut the bottom of the egg carton in half. Lay the plastic over it and push it down into each cup. Use the scissors to poke a hole through the plastic and the bottom of each cup. Make a loop with a piece of yarn. Push about an inch of the loop through a hole. Repeat for all the cups.

3 Spoon some of the seed mixture into each cup. As you work, hold each yarn loop to keep it from slipping out. When all the cups are full, push the wire loop of a metal bell into the top of each cupful of seed mixture.

4 Let the mixture dry for at least four days. Carefully cut away the egg carton. Remove the plastic wrap. You'll have six seed bells. Hang one bell in your bird cage and keep the rest for later. If you don't have a pet bird, hang the bells outside for the wild birds.

MAKE A PROMISE

The best present you can give your dog is a promise. Promise yourself that you will spend at least half an hour each day with your pet. Dogs need more love and companionship than most other pets. Take your dog for a walk to give it fresh air and exercise. Brush the dog's coat to keep it clean. Play with your dog to let it know that it's loved.

Munch-a-Lunch

Tired of eating the same old things for lunch every day? Well, here are some new ideas to try. They're fun to make, and they taste good, too. Three young cooks in San Francisco, California, will show you how to put the recipes together. Just remember to ask an adult's permission to use the stove.

Preparing a batch of trail mix, Milton Wong, 13, carefully measures out a cup of peanuts. Milton and some friends got together in San Francisco, California, to try out some easy-to-make lunch treats.

Chicken Delicious Sandwiches

Marta Mikkelsen, 13, cuts up an apple while bacon sizzles on the stove.

What you'll need:

1 small can of chicken meat, drained, or about 3/4 of a cup of chicken, cut into small chunks
5 strips of bacon (fried, drained on a paper towel, and crumbled)
2 tablespoons apple (peeled, cored, and diced)
3 tablespoons of mayonnaise
3 tablespoons of cream cheese
2 rounds of 5-inch pita bread, sliced in half

Before you begin, let the cream cheese warm to room temperature.

Put all of the ingredients except the bread into a mixing bowl. Stir them well with a spoon.

Divide the chicken mixture into four equal parts. Fill each half-slice of pita bread with the chicken mixture, and top with shredded lettuce, if you wish.

Pita Olé

All hands pat pita olé patties into shape before sliding them into the oven. Later, 13-year-old Megan Kirk samples the finished product (far right).

What you'll need:

4 sliced 5-inch pita bread rounds
1 pound of ground beef
1 egg
1/2 cup of crushed cornflakes (measured after crushing)

1/4 cup of chopped onion
1 package of taco seasoning mix
Break the egg into a bowl. Beat it slightly with a fork. Add the beef, and mix it with the egg. Then blend in the cornflakes, onion, and taco seasoning mix.

Divide the mixture into four equal parts. Flatten each part into a round patty about 1/2 inch thick. Place the patties on a cookie sheet with raised edges. Make sure the patties don't touch each other or the sides of the cookie sheet. Put them in the oven and set the oven at 325 degrees. Bake them for 20 minutes.

Use a spatula to move the patties carefully from the cookie sheet to a paper towel. Cut each patty in half. Then slide each patty half into a half-slice of pita bread. You may want to add shredded lettuce, small tomato chunks, and shredded cheese.

Yummy Treats

Fruit Treat

Using a measuring spoon, Megan scoops partially frozen orange juice concentrate into a measuring cup. The orange juice gives the fruit treat its color and tang.

What you'll need:
1½ cups water
2 tablespoons of quick-cooking tapioca
1 tablespoon of sugar
1/2 cup of orange juice concentrate
2 10-ounce packages of frozen sliced
   strawberries, thawed

Pour the water into a saucepan and add the tapioca. Put the saucepan on the stove and turn the heat to medium. Stir the mixture until it bubbles. Remove it from the heat. Add the sugar and the orange juice concentrate. Stir the mixture and set it aside to cool for 15 minutes. Then pour it into a serving bowl and chill it for at least 30 minutes. Stir in the fruit and serve.

Raspberry Bars

Gently, Milton cuts the butter into the oatmeal-and-flour base for raspberry bars. "Cutting in" means scattering bits of butter throughout the mixture while keeping it crumbly. He does this by pressing the fork through the butter and into the center of the mixture again and again.

What you'll need:
1½ cups of all-purpose flour, sifted
1 teaspoon of baking powder
1/4 teaspoon of salt
1½ cups of quick-cooking oatmeal
3/4 cup of packed light brown sugar
3/4 cup of soft butter or margarine
1 cup of raspberry jam or preserves

Mix the flour, baking powder, and salt in a bowl. Stir in the oatmeal and the sugar. With a fork, lightly blend in the butter or margarine. The batter will look lumpy. Pat 2½ cups of it into an ungreased 11-by-7-by-1-inch glass pan. Spread the jam over the batter. Then cover the jam with the remaining batter. Press the batter down lightly and put the pan into the oven. Set the oven at 350 degrees, and bake the mixture for 30 to 35 minutes, or until it's lightly browned. Set the pan on a cake rack and let it cool, then cut it into bars or squares. Other flavors of jam work, too.

Trail Mix

If you're heading outdoors for a hike or a long bike ride, carry trail mix as a handy snack. It's easy to make. Just mix equal parts of four or five of your favorite dried fruits, nuts, and cereals, and pour them into a sealable plastic bag. If you need suggestions for items to put into your trail mix, try these:

Raisins
Dried fruit
Sunflower
   seeds

Candy-coated
   chocolate bits
Peanuts
Small pretzels

EGG MATCH

People have been decorating eggs for more than 2,000 years. They give the eggs to family and friends as a sign of love and good luck. An artist decorated the eggs at left. She painted two of the eggs carefully, making sure that each detail on one egg was egg-zactly the same as that on the other. She took so much time painting those two eggs, however, that no time was left to make the other four eggs identical to them. Can you pick out the two identical eggs from the rest?

EASTER EGGS-TRAS

SHADOW PLAY

See anything strange about this Easter basket? Its shadow doesn't match it. In fact, there are six parts of the shadow that are slightly different from the basket. Can you spot all six?

JELLY-BEAN JUMP

If you have outgrown the traditional Easter-egg hunt, here's a game that's a little more challenging. It takes only one player. Begin by putting playing pieces, such as pennies, on the squares decorated with jelly beans. Don't use actual jelly beans; they roll around too much.

On your first move, slide one of the playing pieces from its starting position onto any empty space. On each following move, you must jump a piece and remove it from the board. If you play checkers, you know about jumping. You may jump up, down, or across. To win, you must have only one playing piece left.

SHELL SEARCH

If you look only at its surface, a seashell is easy to identify. Each shell has a shape, color, and texture all its own.

If you could look inside a shell with X rays, however, its secret chambers and spiraling tunnels might confuse you.

On these pages, you can see both inside and outside views of a variety of seashells. Can you match each shell with its X ray?

On a piece of paper, make a list from 1 to 10. As you identify each matching shell, write in the shell's letter and name. Below, you can see a completed example.

Beware: There's one X ray with no matching shell, so you can't use the process of elimination.

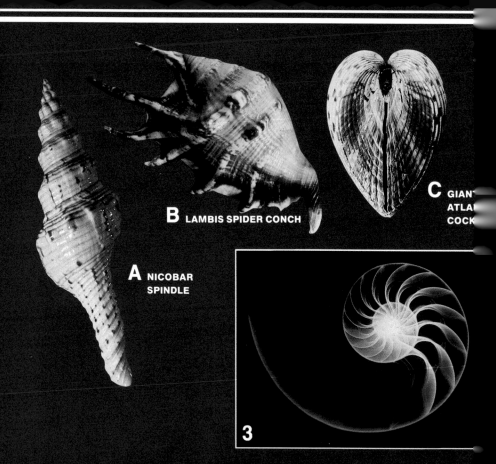

B LAMBIS SPIDER CONCH

C GIANT
ATLA
COCK

A NICOBAR
SPINDLE

3

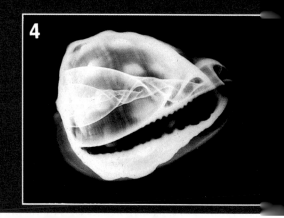

1

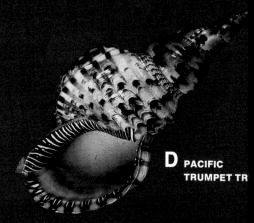

D PACIFIC
TRUMPET TR

2

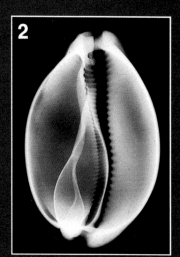

4

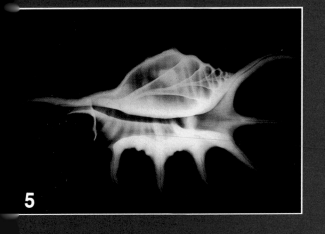

5

F GIANT TUN

G CHAMBERED NAUTILUS

H BULLMOUTH HELMET

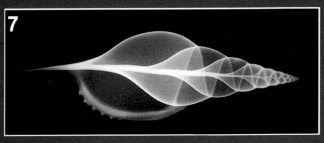

7

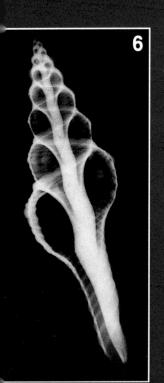

6

8

9

E GOLDEN COWRIE

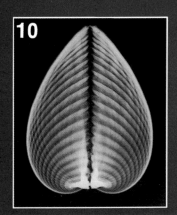

10

I ORANGE SPIDER CONCH

Kitchen Science

The TV's broken? Your magazine subscription's expired? Your friends are out of town? Don't despair. There are a lot of exciting things to do if you just look around — these science tricks, for example.

File Card Magic

Bet a friend that you can put your head through a hole in a 3-by-5 file card — and win! Here's how. Fold the file card in half lengthwise and make 13 partial cuts. Make the first cut through the folded side, the next cut through the other side, and so on. Open the card and cut lengthwise along the fold. Do not cut the two end sections (above). Stretch the card as far as the file cards Mindy and Erin Searcy are holding (right). The secret to this trick comes from a branch of mathematics called *topology*. It teaches that figures can be stretched without changing their area. Mindy, 9, and Erin, 10, live in Orlando, Florida.

Water on a String

Watch water "walk" a string without falling off. Tie one end of a string to the handle of a pitcher of water. Run the string over the spout and hold the other end inside a bowl. Stretch it tight. Hold the pitcher above the bowl and pour slowly and carefully. The water clings to the string because of *surface tension.* Surface tension causes liquids to act as if they were held together by a stretchy, invisible cover.

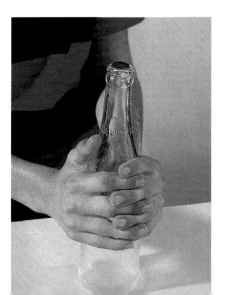

Bouncing Dime

You can make a dime bounce without touching it. Here's how. Put a dime on the top of an empty soft-drink bottle. Wet your finger and run it around the dime and the bottle rim to seal them. Hold the bottle in both hands for about 15 seconds. The dime will slowly move up and down. Heat from your hands warms the air inside the bottle. Warm air expands, pushing up the dime. Now remove your hands. The dime will keep moving until the bottle cools.

Acid-base Test

Many household substances contain acid. You can find out whether things around your house contain acid by conducting this kitchen test. To run the acid test, you'll need these items:

1 red cabbage	Baking soda
Kitchen knife	Two clean bowls
Grater	Water glasses
Strainer	Lemon juice

Now, follow these steps:
1) Cut the cabbage into quarters and grate each quarter, as Susan Rynell, 11, of Bartlett, Illinois is doing (left).

2) Pack the shredded pieces tightly in a bowl and add 1½ cups of hot water. Wait at least an hour.
3) When the water has turned reddish purple, strain it into the other bowl (above). Now your solution is ready.
4) Put some of the cabbage water in the bottom of a glass.
5) Add a little lemon juice. What happens? If the water turns pink (left), the lemon juice is acid.
6) Put fresh cabbage water into another glass. Sprinkle some baking soda into it. Does the cabbage water turn blue as the water on Susan's left did? If so, baking soda is a base, a substance that lessens or neutralizes acid. Now test other items, such as salt, milk, tea, and soap.

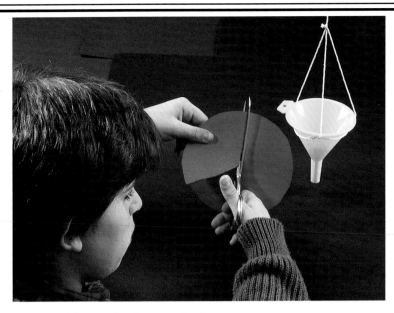

Pendulum Art

If you suspend an object and give it a push, it will move back and forth at a regular rate. Let this action, called *simple harmonic motion*, create some original art on your kitchen table. That's what Bobby Rynell, 11, of Bartlett, Illinois (above), is doing. You'll need these articles.

Small, soft plastic funnel   **Strong string**
Large sheet of black paper   **Scissors**
Cup of salt   **Construction paper**

1) First, make a paper cone to line the funnel. Cut a circle out of the construction paper. Use the bottom of a bowl for a pattern. Remove a quarter of the circle, pull the sides together until they form a cone, and tape them. Leave a small hole at the tip.

2) Tie a string around the lip of the funnel. Use other string to suspend the funnel above the table from a light fixture or the handle of an open cabinet door. The funnel should hang a few inches above the table surface.

3) Place the black paper under the funnel and put the paper cone into the funnel.
4) Block the funnel's tip with a finger and pour in some salt.
5) Remove your finger, push the funnel gently, and let it swing. The salt should form a pattern on the paper.
6) After the funnel stops, pour the salt back into the funnel. Try pushing off the funnel again in different ways and see what other patterns it forms.

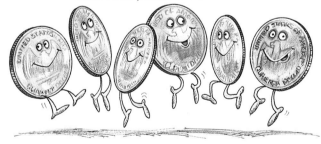

Coin Knockout

Place a stack of quarters or half dollars near the edge of a table with a smooth top. Make sure the coins are stacked evenly. Hold a knife so the blade is flat on the table. With one quick stroke, hit the coin at the bottom of the pile. It will slide out, while the other coins will move only slightly. This happens because most objects tend to stay in place — a principle that scientists call *inertia*.

Grab Bag

For these games, you'll need sharp eyes, along with a pencil and a sheet of paper. If your answers all match the answers on page 103, you're a genuine puzzle whiz.

Can you count all the complete squares on the turtle?

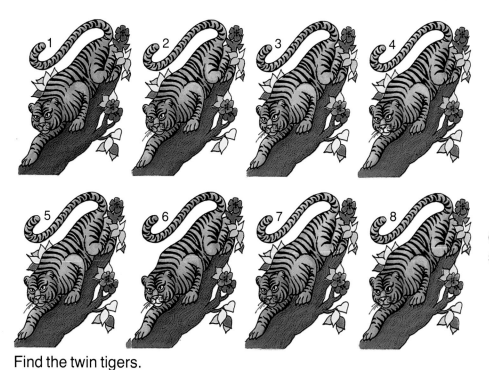

Find the twin tigers.

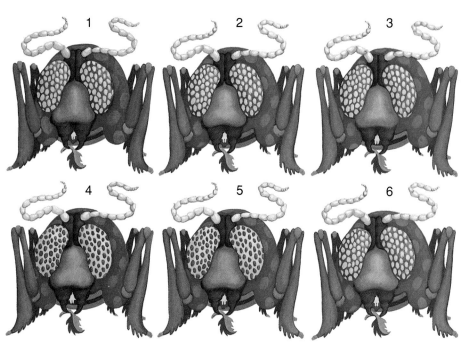

Find the two insects that match.

Draw the ovals and the line without lifting your pencil from the paper. Once you draw a line, you cannot cross it or retrace it.

Find the name of the animal hidden in each of the sentences below. Write the name on a piece of paper.

Example: LONG AGO A TIGER ROARED.

1. THE ARAB BIT INTO THE BREAD.
2. NOBODY CAME LATE TO SCHOOL.
3. I ENJOY EVERY TRIP I GO ON.
4. WILL I ONLY NEED TWO PIECES?
5. BRING A PET TO THE SHOW.
6. HE WILL NOT BE AROUND LONG.
7. EVERYONE PLAYED ON KEY.
8. WHERE HAS WALDO GONE?
9. GRAB AT THE FIRST THING YOU SEE.

Start here

Find nine perfect circles.

This drawing has only one line. Where does it end?

Record - a - Gift

Oops! Your younger sister's birthday is tomorrow, and you're down to your last dollar. Don't panic. Here's an idea for a gift that's inexpensive, fun to make, and will mean more than anything you could buy: a tape recording of her favorite story — complete with sound effects.

What you'll need:
1) One or more tape recorders. If your family doesn't own a tape recorder, you may be able to borrow one from your school or local library.

2) A blank tape.
3) A story. Use a passage from a favorite storybook, find a new one at the library, or make up your own.
4) Household objects to use for making sound effects. There are some ideas on page 89.

Before you begin, prepare a manuscript. Write out the words you will speak in large letters so you can read them easily. Indicate where you want to add sound effects. Then collect what

you'll need to make the sounds. You may want to ask a friend to make the sound effects as you read the story.

Here are other ways to use recordings:
• Ask family members to record their favorite memories of an older relative and send the tape to that relative.
• Record poetry or a short book and send it to a nursing home.
• Write a letter to a relative or a friend who has moved far away and invite family members to help you record it.

SHIP FOGHORN

Partially fill a tall bottle with water. Put the bottle up to your lower lip and gently blow across the top of it. You can make the tone higher or lower by adding or subtracting water.

WAVES ON A BEACH

Pour dried peas or beans into a shallow plastic box. Gently tilt the box from side to side so the peas or beans will roll back and forth.

TEARING CLOTHING

Ask a parent for an old, worn-out section of sheet. Find out where it rips the easiest by testing it along the edges. Then cut a small slit where you plan to make your rip during the recording session.

SPOOKY VOICE

Speak your lines into a metal bucket. The bucket will make your voice echo. To find out how loudly you will have to speak and how far away from the microphone you must stand, run tests with the recorder.

SNORING

Poke a hole in the bottom of a paper cup. Knot a length of braided cord and thread it through the hole from inside the cup. To make a snoring sound, hold the cup in one hand and pull your thumbnail down the cord.

CRACKLING FIRE

Find a crinkly plastic shopping bag of the kind that many department stores now use. Hold the bag near the microphone and crumple it.

GALLOPING HORSE

Bang two insulated plastic thermal mugs on a hard surface. For a gallop, beat a 1-2-pause-3-4 rhythm. To slow the horse down to a walk, beat an even 1-2-3-4 pattern.

THUNDER

Find a thin metal cookie sheet with raised edges on two sides and flat edges on the other two sides. Grip the cookie sheet by the sides with the raised edges and shake the sheet so it bends back and forth.

CAR ENGINE

Record this early. Find a friendly cat. While the cat takes a nap, set up the microphone next to its chest and turn on the recorder. Pet the cat until it begins to purr. Play the sound back as you record your gift tape.

T-Shirt Party

Pillow fights, popcorn, and ghost stories are great, but there are a lot of other ways to have fun when you invite friends to sleep over at your house. Turn your next slumber party into an event to remember. All you need is a little planning and some ideas you'll find here and on the next pages. That's what four friends from Falls Church, Virginia, discovered. The girls, Chrissy Rosholt, 11; Lauren Kramer-Dover and Vicki Spevacek, both 10; and Cristin Brew, 12, played some exciting indoor games. Each also made a souvenir T-shirt to take home and enjoy.

BALLOON RELAY

Grab two balloons and head for the wide open spaces to play balloon relay. Set the balloons at opposite ends of a yard or a big room. Then divide up into two equal teams of three or more players and line up behind the balloons.

After everyone chants together, "One, two, three, go!" the first member of each team picks up the balloon and tucks it under his or her chin. The two players run to the opposite team, tag the last player in line, return, and pass the balloon to their next teammate without using their hands. At right, Chrissy is passing the balloon to Cristin.

The race continues until the first team member on one team receives the balloon again to win the game.

ARE YOU THERE, MORIARTY?

Here's a game that's as much fun to watch as it is to play. You'll need two blindfolds, two long balloons, and a carpeted area with all of the furniture moved aside. You also need a score-keeper. Two people play at one time.

Blindfold the two players and have them lie face down on the carpet with left hands gripping left arms, as Vicki, left, and Cristin demonstrate (below). Give each player a balloon to hold in the other hand. The object of the game is to whack your partner with the balloon.

At a signal, one player calls out, "Are you there, Moriarty (more-ee-ARE-tee)?" The other player answers "Yes," and then dodges quickly to one side as the first player tries to deliver a direct hit on "Moriarty's" head with the balloon.

Each player has five turns at being Moriarty. The player with the most successful hits wins the game.

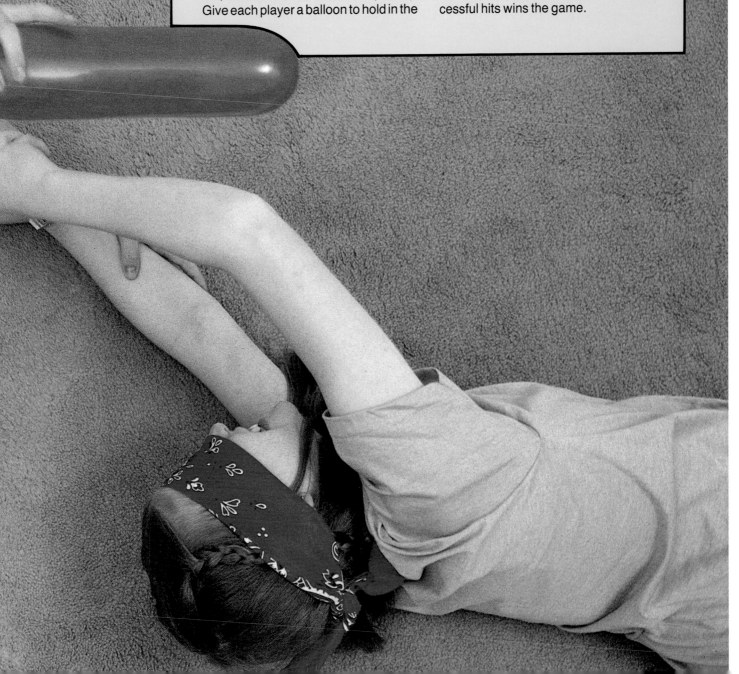

T-SHIRT ART

To make a slumber party really memorable, let everyone design and decorate a souvenir T-shirt. Ask your guests to bring their own T-shirts. You supply a set of fabric crayons. You can buy them at a hobby or craft store. The other items you'll need are paper, straight pins, pencils, and an iron and ironing board. Be sure to ask an adult's permission before using the iron.

First, each guest must draw a design on a sheet of paper. You can make up a design of your own, trace one from a book, or copy one of the designs shown here. Then follow the steps below. (Note: Draw any letters *backward*.)

1) Copy the design on a sheet of paper.
2) Color in the design with the fabric crayons, as Cristin does at left. Make sure you press down hard so a thick coat of crayon wax covers the paper.
3) Slide a sheet of paper into the T-shirt to protect the back of the shirt.
4) Pin the finished design, crayon-side down, onto the front of the shirt.
5) Turn on the iron to the correct setting for the fabric in your T-shirt.
6) Move the hot iron back and forth over the design for several minutes.
7) Carefully unpin one corner of the paper to see if the design is transferring. If not, iron some more until it does.

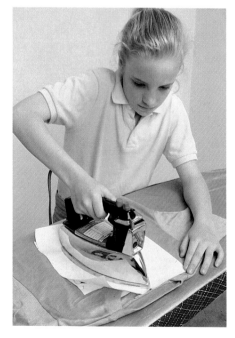

Pressing hard with a hot iron, Vicki waits for the fabric crayon to transfer from a piece of paper onto a T-shirt.

After unpinning one corner, Chrissy and Lauren check their transferring job. The verdict: The colors aren't dark enough. They'll replace the design carefully — so it doesn't shift or blurr — and iron it some more.

The four friends show off their finished souvenir T-shirts.

FOLLOW THAT PATH

How good are you and your friends at giving and following directions? Here's a way to find out. You'll need a blindfold, a sheet of paper at least the size of a piece of typing paper, and two markers of different colors. Blindfold one player. Then draw a line on the paper. The line can bend, twist, and cross itself.

Place the paper in front of the blindfolded player. That player must trace over the line—just by following your spoken directions.

Does this sound easy? It isn't—as Lauren discovers (left).

What in the world...?

What has eyes, but cannot see? On this page, you'll find quite a few
answers to that question. If your own eyes begin to deceive you,
check the answer pages.

*Have a brainstorm and
figure this one out calmly.
You'll go far.*

*Don't get ruffled trying
to guess where these fancy
eyes are found.*

*You're on a roll. If you aren't
glassy-eyed by now, you
can shoot a perfect score.*

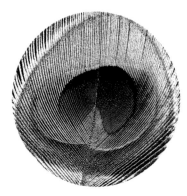

*This eye shows up when a
big, bright bird begins to
strut his stuff.*

*You'll ace the game if you
guess this one — and kick
yourself if you don't.*

*One good turn deserves
another. This hint should
keep you in suspense.*

*You have to uncover a lot
of ground to spy this
eye. How? I'd hoe.*

*If you're sharp, you know
that these don't grow on
trees. Get the point?*

*Poor Susie! Just as she
was beginning to blossom,
she got a shiner.*

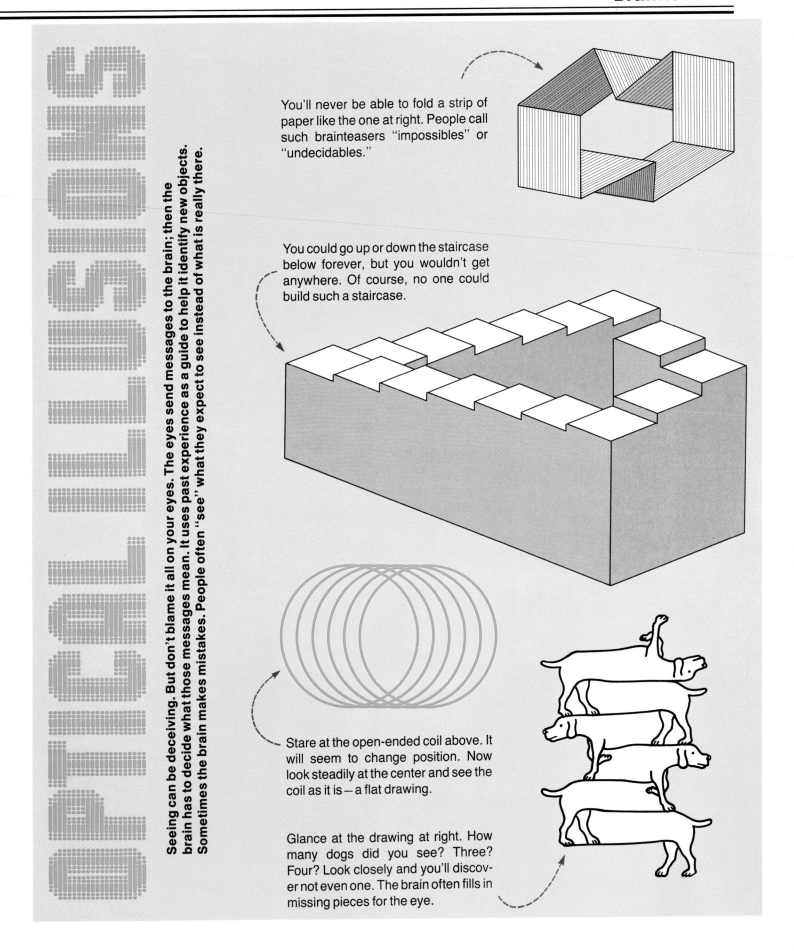

OPTICAL ILLUSIONS

Seeing can be deceiving. But don't blame it all on your eyes. The eyes send messages to the brain; then the brain has to decide what those messages mean. It uses past experience as a guide to help it identify new objects. Sometimes the brain makes mistakes. People often "see" what they expect to see instead of what is really there.

You'll never be able to fold a strip of paper like the one at right. People call such brainteasers "impossibles" or "undecidables."

You could go up or down the staircase below forever, but you wouldn't get anywhere. Of course, no one could build such a staircase.

Stare at the open-ended coil above. It will seem to change position. Now look steadily at the center and see the coil as it is — a flat drawing.

Glance at the drawing at right. How many dogs did you see? Three? Four? Look closely and you'll discover not even one. The brain often fills in missing pieces for the eye.

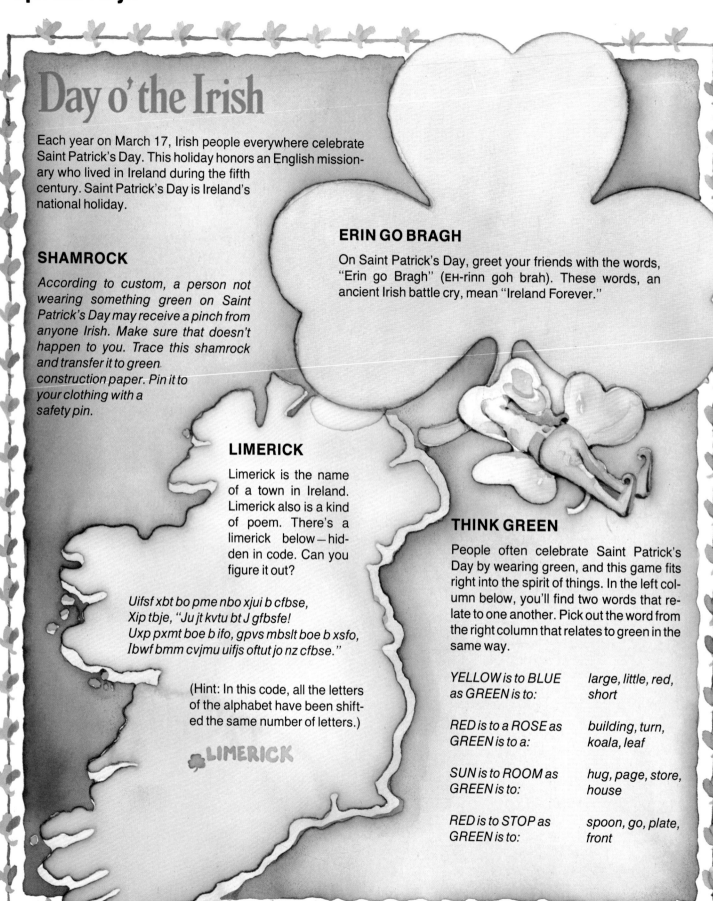

Day o' the Irish

Each year on March 17, Irish people everywhere celebrate Saint Patrick's Day. This holiday honors an English missionary who lived in Ireland during the fifth century. Saint Patrick's Day is Ireland's national holiday.

SHAMROCK

According to custom, a person not wearing something green on Saint Patrick's Day may receive a pinch from anyone Irish. Make sure that doesn't happen to you. Trace this shamrock and transfer it to green construction paper. Pin it to your clothing with a safety pin.

ERIN GO BRAGH

On Saint Patrick's Day, greet your friends with the words, "Erin go Bragh" (EH-rinn goh brah). These words, an ancient Irish battle cry, mean "Ireland Forever."

LIMERICK

Limerick is the name of a town in Ireland. Limerick also is a kind of poem. There's a limerick below—hidden in code. Can you figure it out?

Uifsf xbt bo pme nbo xjui b cfbse,
Xip tbje, "Ju jt kvtu bt J gfbsfe!
Uxp pxmt boe b ifo, gpvs mbslt boe b xsfo,
Ibwf bmm cvjmu uifjs oftut jo nz cfbse."

(Hint: In this code, all the letters of the alphabet have been shifted the same number of letters.)

🍀 LIMERICK

THINK GREEN

People often celebrate Saint Patrick's Day by wearing green, and this game fits right into the spirit of things. In the left column below, you'll find two words that relate to one another. Pick out the word from the right column that relates to green in the same way.

YELLOW is to BLUE as GREEN is to: — large, little, red, short

RED is to a ROSE as GREEN is to a: — building, turn, koala, leaf

SUN is to ROOM as GREEN is to: — hug, page, store, house

RED is to STOP as GREEN is to: — spoon, go, plate, front

WATCH THE ACTION UNDERWATER

Spying on wildlife in a stream, Terry Blosser, 11, of Rockville, Maryland, uses a waterscope she made herself (right). You can make one, too. The drawings below show how.

After you put your waterscope together, take it to a pond or a stream. Hold the plastic-covered end in the water. If the water is clear enough, you'll have a good view of things beneath the surface. You will see even better if your shadow falls on the waterscope.

After a few minutes, you'll probably see things you didn't notice right away. What seem to be flecks or drifting dirt, for instance, may be living creatures.

If you don't see anything after a few minutes, try a different spot. Some parts of the underwater world are livelier than others.

1) *Use a half-gallon milk carton. Cut off the top and bottom as shown by the broken lines above. Tape the bottom edge so the carton won't tear the plastic.*

Clear plastic kitchen wrap will work, but thicker plastic works better.

2) *Cover the bottom and sides with the thickest clear plastic you can find. Use a rubber band to hold the plastic while you tape it to the inside of the open end.*

3) *Tilt the waterscope as you slip it into the water (above). This keeps air from being trapped between the plastic and the water. Don't get water in the open end!*

Thanksgiving Follies

Pilgrims of the Plymouth colony, in Massachusetts, held a huge feast of thanksgiving in 1621 to celebrate their first harvest in the New World. They invited friendly Indians to share the meal.

You may have seen pictures of this famous occasion. But you probably haven't seen a picture that looks like this one. It has several things wrong with it. For example, the woman on the left is wearing a wristwatch.

How many other mistakes can you find? Make a list. Then check yourself by looking at the answer pages.

Animal Crossword

Here's a crossword puzzle that has a whole lot of animals hidden in it, including the ones pictured in the grid. See how quickly you can put all the animals in their proper places.

If you want to save the puzzle to work again later or to share with a friend, put a piece of tracing paper over the puzzle and use a soft pencil that won't leave any marks on the page. You also can copy it on a duplicating machine.

ACROSS

1. Little rodents with long, skinny tails
4. A gander is a male one
6. Short for advertisement
7. Round object
9. Wading bird, often colored scarlet
12. What the sun will do tomorrow morning
13. Animal sometimes called a masked bandit
18. Circus performer
19. Opposite of fast
22. Mammal that can fly
23. What dogs do at the moon
25. Name of a famous killer whale
26. Energy
27. Doglike animal with a long, bushy tail
28. Burrowing animal
31. Largest animals on earth
33. Monkey or gorilla
35. Where 31 across live
36. Female deer
37. Initials of large California city
38. Possess
40. America's First Bird
44. One step for a rabbit
46. Enemy
47. Slice
48. Small child
49. Tiny picnic visitors
52. Go in
53. What poachers break
54. Where a bear lives in winter
55. Sweet potatoes
56. Initials of the smallest state

DOWN

1. Noise a cow makes
2. Taxi
3. TV horse, Mister _ _
5. Largest land animal
8. Red-chested spring worm-catcher
9. Kind of ore
10. Exists
11. Playful mammal with flippers
14. Dull pain
15. Clip-_ _ _ _
16. Old Bossy
17. A silent night hunter
20. Opposite of off
21. State north of OR
22. Bison
24. Save
26. Another name for dad
28. Another name for mom
29. Opposite of new
30. Nickname for lion
31. You and I
32. Half a laugh
34. Cat's hand
35. Climbing rodent with a bushy tail
39. Short sleep
41. To the back of the boat
42. Silly cartoon dog
43. Allow
44. Stalk
45. Sleek river mammal
47. Containers
50. The first word in the name of a country once called Ceylon
51. Opposite of out
52. Aunty in *The Wizard of Oz*

Silly Cyclists

If you think that the scene below looks like fun, study those bike riders more closely. You don't have to be a safety officer to see that a lot of these cyclists are heading for trouble. Some are breaking the law, and some have forgotten to use common sense. How many safety violations can you spot?

CODE-IMALS (Page 6)

From left to right, top row: firefly, fiddler crab, bullfrog

second row: swordfish, sea lion, hedgehog

third row: tiger shark, lionfish, jackrabbit

fourth row: harp seal, barn owl, deer mouse

fifth row: army ants, spider monkey

VALENTINE FUN (Page 7)

HEArts game:

If you found 200 or more words, please be my valentine.

If you found 100-199 words, you've got a lot of heart.

If you found less than 100 words, take out your dictionary and add some more.

Riddle one: Valentine Day always falls after the Fourth of July in the dictionary.
Riddle two: February 14 is the favorite day of the letter V because the letter V is always in love.

APRIL FOOL! (Page 11)

1. Two kinds of molding on cupboard. 2. North American pileated woodpecker head on crane's body. 3. Coffeepot spout upside down. 4. Barbed wire instead of clothesline. 5. Insignia on back of fireman's helmet. 6. Green and red lights reversed on ship's lantern. 7. Beast crouched on upper shelf. 8. Cup not hanging by handle. 9. Electric bulbs growing on plant. 10. Head of little girl on man's bust. 11. Rat's tail on chipmunk. 12. Penholder with pencil eraser. 13. Top of brass vase suspended. 14. Face in clock. 15. Candle where kerosene lamp should be. 16. Sampler dated 1216. 17. Winter seen through left window, summer through right. 18. Antique dealer's head on dolls. 19. Nine branches on traditional seven-branch candelabrum. 20. Girl's hair in pigtail on one side, loose on other. 21. Titles on books vertical instead of horizontal. 22. Girl's sweater buttoned wrong way. 23. Mouthpiece on both ends of the phone. 24. Phone not connected. 25. Goat's head, deer's antlers. 26. No shelf under books. 27. Lace cuff on man's shirt. 28. Five fingers and thumb on girl's hand. 29. Gun barrel in wrong place. 30. Saddle on deer. 31. Potted plant on lighted stove. 32. Girl's purse is a book. 33. Only half a strap on girl's purse. 34. Skunk in girl's arms. 35. Sea gull with crane's legs. 36. Stovepipe missing. 37. Abraham Lincoln with General Grant's military coat. 38. Stove has "April Fool" on it. 39. Hoofs instead of feet on doll. 40. Little girl sitting on nothing. 41. Brass kettle has two spouts. 42. Spur on antique dealer's shoe. 43. Mouse in cabinet. 44. Mouse tracks in wooden floor. 45. Dog's head on cat's body. 46. Raccoon's tail on cat's body. 47. Ball fringe standing straight up at angle. 48. Stove minus one leg. 49. Two kinds of floor. 50. Signature reversed. 51. Last name spelled wrong. 52. Flowers growing in floor. 53. Girl's socks don't match. 54. Girl's shoes don't match.

THINK IT OVER (Page 12)

Starline:

Coin Stack:
1. Dime to C
2. Penny to B
3. Dime on penny
4. Nickel to C
5. Dime on quarter
6. Penny on nickel
7. Dime on penny
8. Quarter to B
9. Dime on quarter
10. Penny to A
11. Dime on penny
12. Nickel on quarter
13. Dime to C
14. Penny on nickel
15. Dime on penny

Odd or Even:

All four answers are true.

STAMP STUMPER Page 14-15

1. A (books)
2. B (mail)
3. C (state names)
4. I (colors)
5. J (coins)
6. H (dogs)
7. G (U.S. Presidents)
8. E (planets)
9. F (relationships)
10. D (hands)

TOP SECRET (Page 23)

Scrambled letters:

Can you do it

Numbers game:

This code is fun

Pigpen:

Pigpen is easy to remember
Enemy coming send more men now

GEOJUMBLE (Page 31)

Answer: ALASKA
1. lake
2. swamp
3. glacier
4. volcano
5. valley

KNOW YOUR GLOBE (Page 32-33)

Check out these fancy cats:
1. Manx
2. Abyssinian
3. Maine coon
4. Russian blue
5. Siamese
6. Burmese
7. Himalayan
8. Persian
9. Scottish fold
10. Turkish Angora

Where in the U.S.A?
1. Massachusetts
2. Wisconsin
3. Louisiana
4. California
5. Alaska
6. Maryland
7. District of Columbia

Map Logic:
423 Cypress Street is spot 7
1156 Second Avenue is spot 9
340 Ash Street is spot 11
1075 Fourth Avenue is spot 1
527 Birch Street is spot 4
1117 Third Avenue is spot 3

GET THIS STRAIGHT! (Page 36)

Missing:
Calendar pages
Sandwich
Milk carton
TV Guide
Cola can
Tennis racket
Crumpled paper
Trash in basket
Yellow note

Moved or returned:
Laundry basket
Jerseys
Coat
Pencils
Books
Crossword puzzle
Glass
Tim's record
Ball
Pink and green notes

Repaired:
Model plane
Trophy

FLOWER POWER (Page 42-43)
1. A
2. G
3. B
4. F
5. I
6. E
7. D
8. C
9. J
10. H

LET'S OBSERVE PASSOVER (Page 48)
Riddles:
1. A magnetic matzo
2. When it is a ruler

U. S. TRIVIA (Page 49)
1. False. General Robert E. Lee was commander of the Confederate Army during the Civil War, which was fought in 1861-1865. The Battle of the Alamo was fought in 1836, as Texas struggled to win independence from Mexico.
2. True.
3. False. Sally Ride was the first American woman in space. As yet, no woman has walked on the moon.
4. False. Dr. Martin Luther King, Jr., was a leader of the Civil Rights Movement during the 1960s. He was assassinated in 1968.
5. True
6. False. Several inventors developed electric light bulbs. Thomas Edison improved on their work when he invented the first practical electric lighting system.
7. False. George and Martha Washington had no children. They lived in New York and Philadelphia during his Presidency (1789-1797). The White House was completed in 1800.
8. False. Charles Lindbergh made the first solo airplane flight across the Atlantic Ocean, in 1927. Wiley Post made the first solo flight around the world in 1933.
9. False. Francis Scott Key wrote "The Star-Spangled Banner" in 1814. Betsy Ross, a seamstress, may have sewn the first official American flag.
10. False. Amelia Earhart was the first woman to fly alone across the Atlantic Ocean, in 1932.
11. True
12. True

FUN-DAY REBUS (Page 50)
When I go to the zoo, I look for the tigers, and picture myself on safari in Asia. Inside their large enclosures, the tigers have room to behave naturally...to stalk and pounce and play.
At the zoo, I also enjoy seeing birds of all colors and sizes. Some live in huge outdoor cages, where they have room to fly, but cannot fly away. They flutter among trees, swim in pools, and build nests.

BRAIN CHECK (Page 54)
Color Mix-up:
From left to right: purple, yellow, red, pink, green

Sock Sort: 3

Stamp Count: 12 (there are 12 in a dozen of anything)

Geometry Test:

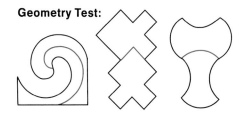

PICK A PUZZLE (Page 56)
Follow This Trail:

Quarter turns:
The quarter makes three complete turns. If you check the answer with real coins, be sure the turning quarter always touches the other coins and does not slip or slide as you move it.

Money Game:
You have $1.19 in coins in your pocket. The coins are a half dollar, a quarter, four dimes, and four pennies.

ROAD SIGNS (Page 62-63)
1. F
2. J
3. A
4. D
5. H
6. K
7. C
8. G
9. L
10. I
11. B
12. E

WHAT IN THE WORLD KINDS OF JOBS ARE THESE? (Page 69)
1. Dog walking
2. Raking leaves
3. Washing cars
4. Baby sitting
5. Plant care
6. Baking

MONSTER MATCH (Page 72-73)
1. Troll
2. Harpy
3. Loch Ness Monster
4. Sphinx
5. Bigfoot
6. Medusa
7. Werewolf
8. Abominable Snowman
9. Cyclops

EASTER EGGS-TRAS (Page 79)
Egg Match:
Starting at top left and counting clockwise, number the eggs from 1 to 7. The matching eggs are 4 and 6. Number 1 has a dot missing; 2 has an odd top border; 3 has a backward leaf decoration; 5 and 7 have missing flower centers.

Shadow Play:
Shadow has:
1. Square handle
2. Bow on wrong side of the handle
3. Only one Easter egg
4. Flower
5. Straight-sided basket
6. Rabbit with only one ear

Jelly-bean Jump:
Make the moves in this sequence:
Slide 8 to 10
Jump 9 to 11
Jump 1 to 9
Jump 13 to 5
Jump 16 to 8
Jump 4 to 12
Jump 12 to 10
Jump 3 to 1
Jump 1 to 9
Jump 9 to 11

1	2	3	4
5	6	7	8
9	10	11	12
13	14	15	16

SHELL SEARCH (Page 80-81)

1-F	6-A
2-E	7-_
3-G	8-B
4-H	9-D
5-I	10-C

GRAB BAG (Page 86-87)

Twin tigers: Tigers 3 and 5 match. Tiger 1 has missing whiskers; 2 and 6 have missing leaves; 4 has a white muzzle; 7 has a missing stripe; 8 has turned eyes.

Insect match: Insects 2 and 6 match. The hind leg of insect 1 has a missing part; 3 has no red on its mouth; 4 and 5 have different spot patterns on their eyes.

Turtle squares: The turtle's shell has 40 complete squares.

Ovals:

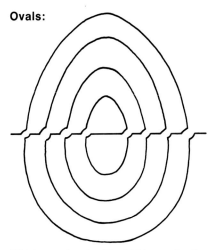

Hidden animals: The hidden animals are: (1) rabbit (2) camel (3) pig (4) lion (5) ape (6) bear (7) donkey (8) dog (9) bat

Nine circles:

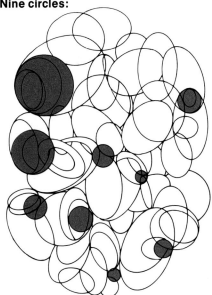

Find the end of the line:

WHAT IN THE WORLD...? (Page 94)

Top row: hurricane, eyelet lace, cat's eye marbles
Middle row: peacock's tail, sneaker, screw eyes
Bottom row: potato, needles, black-eyed Susan

DAY O' THE IRISH (Page 96)
Limerick:
There was an old man with a beard,
Who said, "It is just as I feared!
Two owls and a hen, four larks and a wren,
Have all built their nests in my beard."

Think Green:
Red, leaf, house, go

THANKSGIVING FOLLIES (Page 98)
People at the top, from left to right: first Pilgrim—nurse's cap, safety pin, wristwatch, piggy bank, shower shoes; boy—ice-cream cone, athletic socks, tennis shoes; second Pilgrim—gasoline can, modern hat, bedroom slippers; third Pilgrim—potato chips; first Indian—radio; fourth Pilgrim—catcher's mitt, catcher's chest protector; fifth Pilgrim—modern suit; sixth Pilgrim—peace button on hat; seventh Pilgrim—suspenders. People at the bottom of the picture, from left to right: first Indian—backpack, Band-Aid, cutoff jeans, hamburger and French fries; second Indian—sunglasses, wristwatch. Errors in the rest of the picture: cactus plants, palm tree, electric lamp in window, airplane, ketchup bottle, baseballs in fruit bowl and on table, paintbrushes in pot on table, toaster, fondue pot with candy canes, baseball bat, plastic cup and straws, modern glasses, cups, saucers, plates, and bowls.

ANIMAL CROSSWORD (Page 99)

SILLY CYCLISTS (Page 100)
From back to front: girl running red light; girl riding off curb, girl not giving pedestrian the right of way; boy riding bike that's too big for him, boy riding too close behind car; boy carrying child on handlebars, boy hanging onto car for a tow, girl wearing radio earphones; girl looking back instead of ahead for opening car door, girl riding "no-hands," boy coming out from between parked cars; any bicycle riders not wearing safety helmets.

CONSULTANTS

Nicholas J. Long, Ph.D., *Consulting Psychologist*
Joan Myers, Alexandria City (Virginia) Public Schools, *Reading Consultant*

The Special Publications and School Services Division is grateful to the individuals and organizations listed here for their generous cooperation and assistance during the preparation of A WORLD OF THINGS TO DO: Sandra Bresnick, Hollywood, Florida; Joseph Caravella, National Council of Teachers of Mathematics; Elizabeth Comeau, Arlington County (Virginia) Recreation Department; A. Morris Decker, University of Maryland; Gregory Goldstein, B'nai B'rith/Hillel Foundation; Edwin E. Goodwin, University of Maryland; Theresa Immordino, Peace Corps; Jay Kaplan, National Geographic Society; Conley McMullen, University of Maryland; Erik A. Neumann, U. S. National Arboretum; Andrew F. Pogan, Gaithersburg (Maryland) High School; Hakim Rashid, Howard University; Harald A. Rehder, Smithsonian Institution; Robert K. Robbins, Smithsonian Institution; Jackie Roche, Matthews, North Carolina.

Photography Credits: Phil Schermeister (cover; 4-5, 76-78); Nick Kelsh (2 top left and right, 57-59, 61, 90-93); Günter Ziesler (2 top center, 42 top left); Peter Krogh (3 top left, 30, 44); William DeKay (3 top right, 16-17, 42 F and G, 82, 83 top both, 84-85, 94 top center and right, low center); National Geographic Photographer Joseph H. Bailey (3 low left and right, 20-21, 24-29, 55); Dennis Hamilton, Jr.(8-10); U.S. Postal Service (14-15); Sisse Brimberg (37-39, 97); David S. Boyer, N.G.S. (42 B); Mariette Pathy Allen/Peter Arnold, Inc. (42 C); Stephen St. John, N.G.S. (42 D); Dwight R. Kuhn (42 E and J); Harry N. Darrow/Bruce Coleman Inc. (42 H); Tammy Mobley (42 I); Pamela Zilly (43 #1, 94 center and low left); Norman Owen Tomalin/Bruce Coleman Inc. (43 #2); Tom Stack/Tom Stack & Associates (43 #3); Wayne Lankinen/Valan (43 #4); Alvin E. Staffan (43 #5); © David M. Doody (43 #6); Steve Solum/Bruce Coleman Inc. (43 #7); M. P. Kahl (43 #8); Art Wolfe (43 #9); C. C. Lockwood (43 #10); Kyle McLellan (51); Barry Tenin (62 top right); Keith Gunnar/Tom Stack & Associates (62 center, 63 low center); Virginia Finnegan, N.G.S. (62 low, 63 top left); Nathan Benn (63 top center); Martha Houston-Carroll (63 top right); Robert E. Holland, Jr. (63 center left); © Georg Gerster/Photo Researchers, Inc. (63 center); Lyn Clement (63 center right); Don A. Sparks (63 low left); © Porterfield-Chickering/Photo Researchers, Inc. (63 low right); Barbara Ries (64-67); Alison Wilbur Eskildsen, N.G.S. (69); William A. Conklin/Inner Dimension (80-81); Victor R. Boswell, Jr., N.G.S. (83 low); Defense Meteorological Satellite System, Air Weather Service (94 top left); © Robert P. Carr (94 center left); Anne Heimann (94 center right); Jack Dermid/Bruce Coleman Inc. (94 low right); Animals Animals/Oxford Scientific Films (99 top left); John Shaw (99 top right, low left and low right).

Art Credits: John F. Porter (1); Roz Schanzer (2, 32 top, 33, 36, 45 low, 46, 54, 77-78, 88-89, 100); Barbara L. Gibson (3 left, 6, 12-13, 22-23, 41, 49-50, 56, 58-61, 70-71, 84-85); Marvin J. Fryer (4, 18-19, 67 [Adapted from *The Family Creative Workshop*, Plenary Publications International, Inc., 1976], 92); Dru Colbert (7, 96); Reprinted by permission of the Estate of Norman Rockwell © 1948 Estate of Norman Rockwell (11); D. Mark Carlson, N.G.S. (12 top, 54 low right); Peter J. Balch, N.G.S. (24); Charles W. Berry, N.G.S. (26); Sue Levin (30-31, 40, 68); Joseph F. Ochlak, N.G.S. (32 map, 99); Page 33 game adapted from *The Book of Where or How to be Naturally Geographic* by Neill Bell; Susan Foster (34-35); Robert Cronan, N.G.S. (45 top); Robert Hynes (47); Linda Greigg (48, 79); Page 48 games from *Passover: A Season of Freedom*, Copyright © 1981 by Malka Drucker. Used by permission of Holiday House; Lois Sloan (52-53). Reprinted from Games Magazine (1350 Avenue of the Americas, New York, NY 10019) Copyright © 1985 P.E.I. (54 low); Susan M. Johnston (55, 74-75, 97); Ursula P. Vosseler, N.G.S. (72 lettering); Jeff MacNelly (72-73); Loel Barr (86-87); Shigeo Fukada (95 low right); Robert E. Pullman, N.G.S. and Alfred L. Zebarth, N.G.S. (95); David Earle Seavey (98); Typographic Services (99). Poster front: Robert Hynes
Poster back: Barbara L. Gibson, Sue Levin, and Martin S. Walz, N.G.S.

Library of Congress CIP Data

A World of things to do.

(Books for world explorers ; 8)
Summary: Crafts, activities, games, puzzles, and recipes to suit many occasions, to be done alone or with others.
1. Amusements — Juvenile literature. 2. Creative activities and seat work — Juvenile literature.
[1. Amusements] I. National Geographic Society (U.S.)
II. Series.
GV1203.W84 1987   649'.5   86-31280
ISBN 0-87044-610-X
ISBN 0-87044-615-0 (lib. bdg.)

A WORLD OF THINGS TO DO

PUBLISHED BY
THE NATIONAL GEOGRAPHIC SOCIETY
WASHINGTON, D. C.

Gilbert M. Grosvenor, *President*
Melvin M. Payne, *Chairman of the Board*
Owen R. Anderson, *Executive Vice President*
Robert L. Breeden, *Senior Vice President Publications and Educational Media*

PREPARED BY THE SPECIAL PUBLICATIONS
AND SCHOOL SERVICES DIVISION

Donald J. Crump, *Director*
Philip B. Silcott, *Associate Director*
Bonnie S. Lawrence, *Assistant Director*

BOOKS FOR WORLD EXPLORERS
Pat Robbins, *Editor*
Ralph Gray, *Editor Emeritus*
Ursula Perrin Vosseler, *Art Director*
Margaret McKelway, *Associate Editor*
David P. Johnson, *Illustrations Editor*

STAFF FOR A WORLD OF THINGS TO DO
Margaret McKelway, *Managing Editor*
Alison Wilbur Eskildsen, *Picture Editor*
Ursula Perrin Vosseler, *Art Director*
Patricia N. Holland, *Special Projects Editor*
Barbara L. Bricks, Sheila M. Green, *Researchers*
Eleanor Shannahan, *Contributing Researcher*
Joan Hurst, Nancy J. White, *Editorial Assistants*
Bernadette L. Grigonis, *Illustrations Assistant*

ENGRAVING, PRINTING, AND PRODUCT MANUFACTURE: Robert W. Messer, *Manager;* George V. White, *Assistant Manager;* David V. Showers, *Production Manager;* Timothy H. Ewing, *Production Project Manager;* Gregory Storer, George J. Zeller, Jr., *Senior Assistant Production Managers;* Mark R. Dunlevy, *Assistant Production Manager.*

STAFF ASSISTANTS: Vicki L. Broom, Carol R. Curtis, Katherine R. Davenport, Mary Elizabeth Davis, Rosamund Garner, Donna L. Hall, Mary Elizabeth House, Sandra F. Lotterman, Eliza C. Morton, Cleo Petroff, Virginia A. Williams.

MARKET RESEARCH: Mark W. Brown, Joseph S. Fowler, Carrla L. Holmes, Marla Lewis, Barbara Steinwurtzel, Marsha Sussman, Judy Turnbull.

Composition for A WORLD OF THINGS TO DO by National Geographic's Photographic Services, Carl M. Shrader, Director; Lawrence F. Ludwig, Assistant Director. Printed and bound by Holladay-Tyler Printing Corp., Rockville, Md. Color separations by the Lanman-Progressive Co., Washington, D.C.; Lincoln Graphics, Inc., Cherry Hill, N.J.; NEC, Inc., Nashville, Tenn.